The Macneils of Tokyo

The Annals of the Macneil Clan in Japan

Jack Seward

Tuttle Publishing
Boston • Rutland, VT • Tokyo

First published in 2000 by Tuttle Publishing, an imprint of Periplus Editions (HK) Ltd., with editorial offices at 153 Milk Street, Boston, Massachusetts 02109

Library of Congress Cataloging-in-Publication Data in Process

Distributed by

USA
Tuttle Publishing
Distribution Center
Airport Industrial Park
364 Innovation Drive
North Clarendon, VT 05759-9436
Tel: (802) 773-8930
Tel: (800) 526-2778

Japan
Tuttle Publishing
RK Building, 2nd Floor
2-13-10 Shimo-Meguro,
Meguro-Ku
Tokyo 153 0064
Tel: (03) 5437-0171
Fax: (03) 5437-0755

Canada
Raincoast Books
8680 Cambie Street
Vancouver, British Columbia V6P 6M9
Tel: (604) 323-7100
Fax: (604) 323-2600

Southeast Asia
Berkeley Books Pte Ltd
5 Little Road #08-01
Singapore 536983
Tel: (65) 280-1330
Fax: (65) 280-6290

First edition
06 05 04 03 02 01 00   10 9 8 7 6 5 4 3 2 1

Design by Mary Burgess

Printed in the United States of America

To the Memory of
Anzu

Author's Note

In the 1850s, the first Macneil arrived in Nagasaki to open a business. The trilogy *Annals of the Macneil Clan in Japan* opens with Neil Macneil and continues with his relatives and descendants. *The Macneils of Nagasaki* and *The Macneils of Yokahama* carry the story through the late 1870s.

Historical accuracy is central to these two volumes. Neil Macneil is based on two real-life characters, one of whom, Ranald MacDonald, entered Japan uninvited in 1848 and, while imprisoned in a temple in Nagasaki, managed to become the first teacher of English in Japan. His story is told in *Ranald MacDonald, the First Foreign English Teacher in Japan* by Katherine Plummer, Tokyo YWCA, 1982.

Thomas Glover, the other character, was a respected British merchant, one of the first to establish himself in Nagasaki after the ports of Japan were opened. Glover built one of the largest commercial conglomerates of the time as well as a still-standing mansion said to have been the abode of the fictional Madame Butterfly.

The protagonist in *Nagasaki* and *Yokahama*, Neil Macneil, Sr., is an amalgam of MacDonald and Glover with a generous dollop of the author's imagination—and knowledge of other true-life personalities of those times—mixed in.

The Macneils of Tokyo tells the story of some Macneil descendants and describes their participation in World War II, illuminating events and situations in that war that the author believes have not been given the attention they merit.

The scheme referred to in the story as FEZ—or Far East Zion—was in fact the Fugu Plan, an effort by the Japanese and certain Jews to settle thousands of Jewish refugees from Europe in Manchuria to advance industrialization of that comparatively barren region. One authoritative account is *The Fugu Plan* by Marvin Tokayer and Mary Swartz, Paddington Press, New York, 1979.

A detailed look into the inner workings of Radio Tokyo is offered, including a more truthful account of Iva Toguri D'Aquino's work there than has been offered previously. Known in America and to GIs who served in the Pacific Theater as "Tokyo Rose," she was an outspokenly pro-American woman who refused to renounce her U.S. citizenship throughout the war. Her postwar imprisonment was unjust and her subsequent pardon by President Gerald Ford was overdue. If any Japanese-Americans should have received compensation for what befell them, D'Aquino should have been the first. Of several books written about her, two are reasonably factual.

Intertwined into *Tokyo* is a subplot describing Japan's development of atomic weapons. A reliable history can be found in *Japan's Secret War* by Robert K. Wilcox, William Morrow, New York, 1985. Readers may be amazed to discover how close the U.S. forces came to being targets of Japanese atom bomb attacks in the final days of the war.

According to page 6 of the *Military Press* of July 1, 1989, Japan test-fired an atomic weapon one day after we dropped "Fat Man" on Nagasaki. In *Tokyo*, I advanced that date slightly for the sake of the story.

With five cyclotrons and a good source of "heavy water" in Konan, Korea, Japan was capable of moving ahead quickly with bomb construction and might well have had half a dozen smaller bombs ready when the Allies landed on the beaches of Kyushu in November. Had that happened, what would the Japanese have to say today about those who used the bomb on them? Would they have become the "barbarians" for having used these weapons, as Americans became to many of them?

The Baron Nobutaka Matsui in the novel was inspired by, and bears a loose resemblance to, Baron Takeichi Nishi. He also drove a gold-painted, 12-cylinder Packard and on his horse, Uranus, won an Olympic medal in 1932. Otherwise, my Matsui bears little similarity to history's Nishi.

Only a few true names are used, but the courageous exploits of our Allied Translator and Interpreter Service teams in the South Pacific are depicted in a way that should reflect kindly on reality and on the Nisei and Caucasian team members, many of whom I have been pleased to count as friends.

About the war in the Pacific itself: the battles, invasions, places, dates, and military units are authentic. The leading admirals and generals, as well as some colonels and majors, are historical personages.

The Macneils of Tokyo might be called an historical (and romantic—for love is at its heart) adventure novel, whose setting is World War II and whose perspective is American. All the Macneils are very much alive in my imagination.

Jack Seward
Houston, Texas
Summer 1999

The Macneils of Tokyo

chapter 1

Tokyo, Japan
August 1941

The aging American at the head of the table raised his glass.

"To the Macneils!" Even as he spoke, he wondered sadly when, and even whether, the family's next annual banquet would be celebrated.

The man's older son, Bill Macneil, frowned but remained silent while slowly raising his own wineglass. The only daughter, the effervescent Sarah, cried, "The Macneils forever!"

Shipton ("Ship") Macneil, only fourteen, added shyly, "To us," then said, "I wish Mother could be here."

"We'll all go upstairs and visit her later, if that damned nurse will let us," grumbled the clan patriarch.

The butler entered to ask if the servants could begin serving the noon meal.

"Have them wait about five minutes, Fukai-san, and close the door when you leave." Even at seventy-one, Neil Macneil was stiffly erect with a full head of hair and a commanding presence enhanced by a voice that had lost none of the impressive timbre of its prime. When he spoke, others listened with the respect usually paid to vast wealth.

After the senior of the family retainers of the clan—the Macneils still thought themselves more clan than family—softly closed the dining-room door, Neil Macneil, illegitimate son of a pioneer merchant of the same name and that merchant's first cousin Anne, waited for the attentive silence of his three children. Then he began.

"My annual report on the state of our fortunes is disheartening."

"Are we broke?" the infectious Sarah asked, almost as if she welcomed the prospect of new adventures coarsened by poverty.

Her father grinned wryly. "You know we're not, my dear. I've had a summary of our financial condition prepared. Copies will be given to each of you later. As usual, read, digest, and destroy. As you will see, we own less than last year, but we're far from destitute. Anyway, that's not why I wanted us to have this private talk."

Bill Macneil squared his shoulders. "You want to talk about the coming war, don't you, Dad?"

The father smiled at his son. He could always rely on Bill to know what was on his father's mind.

"And I'm almost glad it's coming," Bill muttered.

Neil Macneil well knew the reason behind his son's mumbled comment.

"Yes, a war is inevitable. I've sold too many arms to too many nations not to read the omens. I can hear bugles, even if others won't. Since the Macneils can do nothing to prevent this conflict, we must prepare for it." Although no one but family was present in the dining room, the patriarch lowered his voice. "I intend to shift all our liquid assets out of Japan. In fact, out of Asia entirely. Our main office will move to the United States: New York, maybe San Francisco. I'll sell as much of our real estate as I can as well as our holdings in Japanese corporations."

"What about us?" Sarah asked. Twenty-one, she had spent the previous summer in the Dairen, Manchuria, branch of Macneil Brothers' Trading Co. Petite, intelligent, Sarah seemed always to be in motion, flitting from one enthusiasm, one cause to another. Her father thought of her as a breeze of compassion, blowing hither and yon seeking yet another of the afflicted on whom to lavish sympathy and support. Her amah, Mrs. Chang, said the girl she had raised since birth would swim a flooded river to tend an injured mouse.

"You children have no financial concerns, Sarah. The main thing is to go where you will be safe. Bill is returning to school in San Francisco next week. I trust Ship and I and your mother will leave Japan by the end of the year or early next year. And you had better not stay in Manchuria much longer."

"But Daddy," Sarah protested, "I don't want to be separated from Nathan. Not until he can leave Manchuria with me. Besides," she added with a quick smile, "I'm sure there won't be a war. Both of you are always so pessimistic."

"What about you?" Shipton Macneil asked his father.

Neil Macneil grinned. "It's about time for me to retire, don't you think? After all, I'm seventy-one. Your mother and I will go to Oregon and find a quiet place to enjoy life. Somewhere close to a hospital for her."

"But can Mother travel?"

With Ship, his father thought, it was his mother first, last, and always. A delicate boy but with definite inner strengths. "I think she can make the trip."

"If she can't, I'll stay here with her," Ship declared.

Although much younger than her husband, Umeko had been an invalid for six years. "If a war starts, Son, you might have to change citizenship in order to stay." But Neil Macneil really didn't think it would come to that. Surely, he could get Ship and Umeko out of Japan in good time.

All three children and he carried American passports. Although the Macneil clan, at least the Japan branch of it, had established itself in Japan in the 1850s. Except for the invalid Umeko, they had always considered themselves American. Everyone spoke and wrote Japanese as well as, maybe even better than, English. All had received much of their education in Japanese schools. They thought in Japanese as often as in English, and Japanese friends probably outnumbered American and European ones.

Even so, they insisted on retaining their identity as Americans. Fellow Americans back home might look at them askance, but nothing could ever shake a deeply held belief that they were as American as youngsters who had been born in and never left Olathe, Kansas.

"Oregon?" Bill asked in reference to his father's plan to retire there, "Why Oregon?"

"It's where your grandfather came from."

"Right," Bill mused. "I'll have to drive up some weekend from San Francisco and see what old Fort Stockton looks like."

His father smiled. "You won't find any trace of the original Macneil trading post, I'm afraid."

"That's a shame, Dad. I'd have liked seeing it." Bill shifted his attention to his sister. "Speaking of disappearing trading posts, Sarah, Dad's right. If war starts, Manchuria is the last place you want to be."

"But what about my job in our office?" she asked with intentional deception. "How can they possibly manage without me?"

"Cut it out, sis. We all know why you want to be there," Bill bantered in the tone he often used with his younger sibling.

"All right, I admit it," Sarah said, laughing. "I'm in love.

Madly, wildly in love. Nathan Blum is the most marvelous man. Gentle, intelligent, so dark and . . ."

"Why do women prefer dark men?" Bill asked with mock petulance. He and his father were blond, as was Bill's long-dead mother, Valerie. Neil's second wife was Japanese, so Sarah and Shipton were Eurasian or, more properly, Amerasian.

"I sometimes suspect you don't like Nathan because he's a Jew," Sarah said, suddenly turning pugnacious.

"Oh, I don't mind his being a Jew, but he's too smooth a talker and—well, a bit too refined for my taste," Bill said, happy to deliver tit for tat.

"You think he's more interested in our money than in me? Well, let me set you straight, dear brother of mine. His father owns most of the movie theaters in Dairen."

"As well as most of the opium dens, gambling halls, and good-time houses."

As Sarah's cheeks flushed, her eyes kindled with the fires of confrontation. "Money's money, no matter where it comes from, Bill. I'll bet your sweet little Miss Bluestocking Quaker would die to have some of ours, too. Talk about setting your cap for a rich husband!"

"If you're talking about Helma Graf, you can stop worrying, Chankoro." That was the family's pet name for Sarah, somewhat analogous in Japanese to the English pejorative "Chink."

Why the family called Sarah "Chink" was another story.

"When I board my ship in Yokohama next week," Bill went on, "I hope I will have seen the last of her. Besides, she despises wealth as much as she does war and our family arms business. She's altogether rabid on the subject."

"Is that the hogwash she's been feeding you?"

"Lay it to rest, Chankoro. Helma's greed or lack of it is not the issue. There's a lot more involved."

chapter 2

Tokyo, Japan
August 1941

Neil Macneil switched on the ceiling fans in his study, settling himself into the coolness of his leather chair to wait for his daughter.

Sarah was a truly fine woman, he thought with a father's complacency. If not for her febrile compulsion to sacrifice herself for impossible causes, he would have had few reservations about her.

It was odd how three children with the same father could be so utterly different. Ship was weakest, yet strong in support of those things he really believed in. By contrast, Bill—on whom rode the clan's hopes for the future—was strong, yet weak in allowing his resentment over what had happened in Nanking in 1937 to hold him in its stubborn grip.

And Sarah: always smiling, ever serene, eager to please, ready to protect, impossible to dislike. Her personality overwhelmed her beauty in a viewer's eyes, but if one should be so fortunate as to chance upon her sleeping, then it was her beauty—the oval face, exquisite daintiness, hair as black as a crow's wing, large dark upturned eyes, long lashes, perfect nose and lips—that made a viewer yearn to tarry and drown in her loveliness.

What was so perplexing about Sarah's comeliness was that no one could say with conviction if it was Oriental or Occidental or, if even part Oriental, what kind of Oriental. Without doubt her bloodlines were Scot and Japanese. Her birth registration vouched for that. But hers was one of those rare, rare faces that only provided hints, without certainties. Olive-skinned and dark-eyed, yes, but those could have been Hispanic genes. A petite French physique with a Spanish dancer's lithe body. Hair of ebony, but there were the Black Irish.

Old Japan hands like Macneil could always tell at a glance whether a person was Korean or Chinese or Japanese, but with Sarah it would have been hard even for him to decide. Chinese? Maybe. Japanese? Possibly.

Sarah's grandfather, her mother Umeko's illustrious father, had been Japan's ambassador to China for many years. Umeko had given birth to Sarah in her father's embassy in Peking, where her birth was recorded in Chinese records. A Chinese amah-san, Mrs. Chang, had soon been employed to care for Sarah as her own. Sarah's first language was Chinese, and she had a Chinese name: Lin Hsiao-mai. When she was brought to Japan and began to grow up with Bill and later Shipton, it was perhaps inevitable, in the cruel way of siblings, that they would come to call her Chink, or Chankoro.

When Sarah entered her father's study, she walked over to perch on the arm of his chair and kissed his forehead. The gesture worried Macneil, since it presaged a request that would not be easy to grant. Sarah had wanted to talk to him in private for three days, but he had put her off on one pretext or another until now, and time was running out.

"I love you, Daddy," she whispered.

"How much do you want?" he asked, pretending to reach for his wallet.

"Stop teasing," she said, ruffling his greying hair. "Why do you think I want your money?"

"Don't you?"

"Of course not." Sarah moved from her father's easy chair to one nearby.

"But there is something I want," she added.

"I knew it," he said, forcing a frown onto his face.

"Please, Daddy," she said, moving to the edge of her chair. "This is something I want more than I have ever wanted anything. Now that Nathan and I are engaged, I—"

"Engaged?" She had startled him. "Since when?"

"Well, we won't announce it till next month, but that's the way we feel about each other, so I figure it's like being engaged already."

She blew a conciliatory kiss at her father. "I want to help Nathan with a plan he and his father have. It's about a homeland for the Jews in the Far East."

"Great Jesus, Sarah, what the hell are you about to get yourself into?" For the first time, true alarm colored Macneil's expression.

"Daddy, I want him to tell you. He's much more persuasive than I am."

Macneil was still disgruntled. "At least give me an idea."

"I'll tell you this much: There are about sixteen thousand Jews in Manchuria now. Mostly refugees. Japan wants to populate Manchuria, right? But not many Japanese want to immigrate there. It's a cold, empty land, but one with immense natural resources. Now, if Japan could persuade fifty or even a hundred thousand Jews to go there from Europe, they could build up Manchuria as an industrial base. The Jews who are being so mistreated in Europe would have a permanent home and would bring with them skills and maybe even some capital. Japan, and American Jews, would provide more. The Blum family plans to invest several million, so if the Macneils would become involved . . ."

Amazement was clear on Macneil's features. "Chankoro, do you really have any idea at all what you're talking about?"

"Don't call me Chink."

"All right then: Little Sarah." Macneil leaned forward and grasped one of her hands between his. "To help fifty or a hundred thousand Jews migrate to Manchuria and build plants for them to work in and homes for them to live in would cost hundreds of millions of dollars. If the Japanese government wants to support such a project, let them put up the money."

Sarah reacted. "The Japanese supporters of this plan are several men in the foreign ministry and some navy officers. There's considerable support for the idea, but there's opposition, too, Daddy. Even the Japanese who like the idea, including the president of the South Manchurian Railway, want to do it on the cheap. They think rich American Jews should put up most of the capital. Nathan wants our family and his to put up—what did he call it?—the 'seed money.'"

"What's in it for us?"

"I wish you would not think of it in that crass way, Daddy."

"I have no choice. We've already lost a lot of money in the past two years, and we are going to lose a lot more in this war. Even if I believed in this plan wholeheartedly and loved all the Jews in the world, the Macneils could not invest enough to make any difference. We have resources, but we're not that rich."

"Nathan is determined to plunge ahead."

"And I suppose you are, too?"

"I love him, Daddy. With all my heart."

"This plan: What does your Nathan Blum call it?"

"He calls it FEZ: Far East Zion."

"Jesus Christ in the Andes, Chankoro! You've bitten off one hell of a mouthful this time. I didn't mind when you wanted to buy a ranch to keep those cattle that escaped from the slaughter house in Shinagawa. Or your opening a refuge for stray cats. Or even your building a home for battered wives in Chiba. But this is too much, girl."

"At least, will you let me use my own money?"

Macneil thought for a moment. "I might let you have an advance against your inheritance. Maybe a few hundred thousand dollars. More, once I can get our liquid assets into dollars and out of Japan."

"I'll take it," Sarah said sweetly, rising.

"Hold on a minute. I'll want to know a lot more about the exact details of how you're going to invest that money."

"Daddy, remember, I'm twenty-one now," she said, with a dangerous glint in her eyes.

"How well I know." Macneil shook his head ruefully. "Still, I want to talk to your Nathan Blum about this. Even if I don't invest any of my money, at least I can give him some advice."

"I'll arrange it, but we'll have to hurry. Mrs. Chang and I are sailing for Dairen in a few days."

"Remember, you'll have to cultivate all the Japanese support for—FEZ?— you can get. I suppose I can get you an introduction to Mister Aikawa of the South Manchurian Railway."

"Wonderful! You're such a dear. I've already begun circulating in Japanese society there. I've got two colonels and even a general who are obviously interested in a lot more than my sweet smile."

"Sarah, I do not like the sound of that."

"Don't worry, Father dear. I'll tell you in confidence what Nathan says about me: 'Always on the verge, but still a virgin.'"

"God, I hope so."

Sarah shielded her eyes against the burning afternoon sun. She waited impatiently for one of the drivers to bring a family car around from the garage.

The chauffeur was a middle-aged man she had not seen before, but Sarah resisted her natural impulse to engage him in a conversation. After telling him to take her to the Imperial Hotel in Hibiya, Sarah sat back, closed her eyes, and immersed herself in impatient thoughts about her lover.

Only two years older than she, Nathan Blum had returned from the Conservatoire de Musique in Paris earlier in the year, when she had first met him.

At once he had begun an ardent pursuit of Sarah. If he had not, she would have pursued him. Nathan was delicate and sensitive and quiet, and she longed to hold him in her arms and nurture him. His longish hair and intense eyes suited the image of what he burned to be: a concert pianist. His flexible fingers fascinated her as they danced over the piano keys. Those same fingers caressing her bared breasts sent a lovely thrill into her nether region, where those nimble hands had yet to be admitted.

Nathan was courtly and reserved. There was an unmistakable Gallic elegance about him. Although he and his father held French citizenship papers, Nathan was born in Manchuria and spoke French as his native language, good Mandarin Chinese, but utterly inadequate English. He and Sarah conversed in Chinese, which raised curious eyebrows when they were overheard in public speaking the Peking dialect.

Nathan Blum had not become the concert pianist he longed to be. He could never bring himself to practice more than two hours a day, even as his teachers at the conservatory assured him a minimum of four ("Four, *M'sieu* Blum, *four!*") was necessary. They could have added, but charitably did not, that even more essential was a natural talent for the keyboard, which they privately feared had not been bequeathed to Nathan by his Creator.

After a vacation at his home in Dairen, Nathan Blum had intended to return to Paris and his studies, but then he met Sarah "Chink" Macneil, known to her Chinese friends as Lin Hsiao-mai.

Nathan played on the strings of Sarah's heart with a skill and devotion he had never addressed to the keyboard. She had responded by falling passionately, exhilaratingly in love. It was as if all the affection and devotion Sarah had ever lavished on abused wives, desperate cattle, lost kittens, and fallen sparrows had focused on a single person—the slim, aesthetic Jew, Nathan Blum.

CHAPTER 3

Yokohama, Japan
August 1941

The freighter's cranes whirred and creaked, the second mate roared commands, the stevedores shouted at each other, and the August afternoon sun peeled more paint off the ship's strakes. If the 7,800-ton vessel was to clear the bay's crowded entrance before dark, the master would have to push all hands to their limits.

Reclining against a stanchion on the main deck, Bill Macneil hoped they made it. His schedule was flexible, but the sooner he left this country he had come to dislike so intensely the better. In fact, if the Macneil Lines' *City of Glasgow* could cast off its mooring lines from the dock bollards and stand out to sea this instant, it would not be too soon for Bill Macneil. Then he could have avoided what was sure to be a painfully awkward parting with Helma Graf.

"Excuse me, Mister Macneil." The stubby, white-haired captain stood beside Bill, touching the enameled visor of his white hat with two fingers. "I regret we don't have an owner's cabin aboard these freighters, sir, but I don't think we've ever had the pleasure of having a Macneil aboard. Is your cabin satisfactory? I'd be glad to let you have mine, but it would be tomorrow before I could have it cleaned and ready for you."

Bill Macneil smiled. "The accommodations are quite all right, Captain. Tell me, when do you expect to slip lines?"

Captain Davis cast a judicious eye at the heaps of cargo still on the dock, then at his pocket watch. "Not for at least three or four hours."

"In that case, I believe I'll take a quick ride up to the Bluff."

"Your family once had homes up there, didn't they?"

Bill nodded. "And if a Miss Helma Graf comes looking for me, ask her to wait in my cabin, will you? And turn the fans on in there, please."

The captain saluted. "I'll tell the steward to place a block of ice in front of one of the fans, sir."

Bill Macneil felt in his pants pocket for his passport and wallet, then strode down the gangplank. Taxicabs would be waiting along the Bund only 75 yards away. He lengthened his stride.

At twenty-two, Bill Macneil was an easy-moving natural athlete with not the slightest interest in competitive sports. He could do twenty-five one-armed push-ups, twist around and catch an oncoming baseball behind his back, and pass a football as well with his left as his right arm, but he did such feats only when begged to do so by children.

His sister, Chankoro, called him "sports-deaf." Perhaps he was. He did not know the name of the lead pitcher for the New York Yankees or remember which football teams had played in the January 1941 Rose Bowl.

Bill's only sport was mountain climbing, which he did not consider competitive. After learning to fly at fields around San Francisco, he had taken up mountain climbing in northern California and Oregon, where he joined a team that rescued amateur mountaineers stranded in the high peaks. When Bill's team failed to climb up to one couple in time, the four members decided to add parachuting to their skills.

Over the past two years of Bill's attendance at the University of San Francisco, he had answered eleven distress calls from the northern mountains.

Despite a break in his right ankle bone on his sixth jump, Bill had persevered, and now nothing gave him more satisfaction than flying his own plane to a field near the origin of the distress call, joining the rescue team, and parachuting in when necessary to save endangered and sometimes injured climbers.

That was the extent of his athletic activity.

The ankle fracture still sent occasional twinges up his right leg—it did now as he climbed the slope from the Foreigners' Cemetery on the Bluff to the site of the two homes built long ago by Macneils as their Yokohama residences.

This pilgrimage had no particular objective. Probably no member of his family had bothered to come up here in years, although they still owned the land. Perhaps, he thought, someone should come up now and then to pay respects to the past.

His grandfather had built a house right over there on the left of the narrow road in the 1870s, and his grandmother had built another next door the following year. Neither had really been permanent. What was considered the main family residence still stood empty in Nagasaki, while Grandmother Anne had possessed two in Tokyo. From all he had heard, she must have been quite a woman. Imagine, a Scotswoman long imprisoned by the Japanese becoming first the teacher of the emperor, then his occasional mistress.

The Yokohama homes were destroyed in the Great Kanto Earthquake of September 1923 and never rebuilt. By then almost all Macneil affairs, especially the arms business, were conducted from the Tokyo main office. The rest, certain commodities like ships, steel, and tea, were exported from Nagasaki.

After standing in front of the property for several minutes, Bill Macneil shook his head and grinned wryly. Face it, he thought, the real reason for coming up here on this hot and muggy late summer afternoon was the urgent desire to avoid Helma Graf. He hoped she would come aboard the *City of Glasgow* while he was on the Bluff, get tired of waiting, and return to her missionary parents' home in Shizuoka, on the south flank of Mount Fuji. A good hour and a half by train.

Turning, he started down the slope where he had left the taxi. One of the few things he still liked about Japan was these vehicles for hire. A person could rent one of them for an entire day for the equivalent of two or three American dollars.

He really shouldn't treat Helma so cavalierly. She deserved better than he could bring himself to provide. After all, her only sin, if it was one, was to have set her cap for him.

The driver dozed at the wheel of the black made-in-Japan Ford. Macneil touched the man's shoulder to rouse him, then climbed in back. "Return to the dock," Bill said, ignoring the driver's surly glare.

He let his mind review Helma's good qualities, of which she surely had a share. She was mentally acute, shy, pensive, and modest. Modest to a fault, in fact, befitting a daughter of Quaker missionaries from the German-speaking region of Switzerland. She had a trim figure, kept well-concealed in chaste outfits. Despite her education at Bryn Mawr College in the United States, so far she had avoided some of the independent, willful ways that were making American women the envy and despair of other women. Only in support of the tenets of her religion—peace, nonviolence, brotherly love—did Helma's alpine blue eyes flash and her gentle, normally subdued voice take on dangerous undertones.

Bill Macneil had no way to judge the quality of her spoken French or her German, but he knew her English was nearly perfect, as it should be, he thought, since Helma had received much of her earlier education in the United States as well as college. Her fluency in Japanese, however, was another matter. Since joining her parents in Japan, Helma had expended massive efforts to learn Japanese. But it was not a language to be learned in one or two years. Having grown up speaking Japanese, Bill Macneil had little concept of what was actually involved in learning the language in school, but he had known more than a few Americans who had lived in this country for ten years or longer who had finally thrown up their hands in frustrated despair at ever coming to grips with the language. One early missionary had reported to Rome in despair that Japanese must have been devised by Satan to thwart the dissemination of God's holy word.

In fact, Bill had met the then, twenty-year-old Helma Graf for the first time early that summer in the town of Manazuru on the Izu Peninsula. On a side street, she had been trying to tell a group of some two dozen casually interested Japanese about her religious beliefs. Preaching in rural towns like Manazuru was part of her training to follow in her parents' footsteps as missionaries.

The problem, Bill Macneil quickly realized, was that her

audience did not comprehend what she was trying to get across to them. Helma had the vocabulary, but her grammatical structures were shaky and her pronunciation execrable.

At first he was amused, but then pity for the charming and determined young woman began to take over. She was trying valiantly, but her Japanese listeners were beginning to giggle as Japanese often do when confronted with foreigners who mangle their language.

Pushing through the small crowd to Helma's side, Bill smiled at the puzzled, tittering audience and began speaking to them in calm, persuasive Japanese, the native fluency of which fetched gasps from some. Probably none had ever heard an American speak Japanese that was little different, though possibly better, than their own.

"Please forgive my sister. She has only recently come to your beautiful country and needs a few more months of language study.

"What she wants to say to you is that all the world's people should love one another. They should open their hearts and be understanding and sympathetic." Macneil was interpreting Helma's words pretty much as she had tried to express them. "Brotherly love and nonviolence are the keys of our religion. We call ourselves the 'Friends' because that is what we truly want to be: your friends." Macneil went on with his understanding of Helma's message. Later, she would expound those principles to him often.

The small audience accepted readily enough Bill's claim to be Helma's brother. There was, in fact, a strong resemblance between the two. Bill knew the saying: Opposites attract. Maybe that was their trouble. They were too much alike. The same blond hair and light blue eyes. Mobile lips. Oval faces. Where they differed most was inside: in philosophy, beliefs, attitudes. And in how they viewed the Japanese. Helma loved them, as she professed to love all people. However, despite the affection Bill felt for his Japanese relatives and friends, he despised the people of Japan en bloc, especially the arrogant, cruel men. This was not a casual difference of opinion between him and Helma. It was a chasm deep as the Grand Canyon, into which Bill had actually parachuted in March 1941.

After their reasonably successful, albeit impromptu, revival meeting, Bill Macneil had taken Helma Graf aside and introduced himself. She thanked him courteously and agreed to have tea with him in a shop near Manazuru Station. In her quiet, insistent way, she overwhelmed him with questions about himself: his ability in Japanese, his inspiration to come to her aid, why he was in Manazuru. Bill wondered if she considered him a possible convert to the peaceable persuasions of the Friends.

After her torrent of questions, Helma retreated into the stillness Bill was to find so characteristic of her. Quiet, watchful, contemplative, always peering into the souls of others. That contagious serenity made the most lasting impression on him.

Helma's waters ran deep indeed, and he was only beginning to discover their depths.

Yet her passions were surprising for a daughter of missionaries. Her favorite song was "I'm in the Mood for Love," which she hummed and whistled to his distraction. She was addicted to the tango and had twice prevailed on Bill to take her to a Tokyo nightclub called the Florida, known in Japan as the 'home of the tango'. Her dance steps had been so smooth and skillful that Bill soon quit the floor to let one of the instructors employed by the club dance three tangos with her. One, Helma's favorite, was "Ein Spanischer Tango." Bill led the applause after her performance.

The taxicab stopped on the Bund and was dismissed by Macneil.

On this miserably hot afternoon, Bill Macneil did not relish what he would have to say to Helma.

chapter 4

Yokohama, Japan
August 1941

Bill Macneil stopped on the main deck to cool off in the shade of the number four lifeboat. Here, at least, he could feel a breeze off Tokyo Bay. His cabin, even with the benefit of fans and ice, might, at best, be considered tolerable.

Besides, he wanted to collect his thoughts before what would most likely be an emotional scene with Helma Graf.

Glancing toward the end of the dock where it joined the Bund, Bill spotted a tall, erect, slow-moving Caucasian. For a moment, he thought the man was his father come to bid him goodbye, but then knew it was not. Bill had not really expected Neil Macneil, Jr. to travel the 33 miles to Yokohama in this summer heat. They had said their farewells at the Azabu residence, and they were on the chilly side because of their recent harsh words of disagreement. The two men had stopped just short of shouting at each other, the first time in Bill's memory he and his father had engaged in a near-violent argument. In time they would apologize and forget, but the words of the dispute smoldered in Bill's mind.

Their conflict came down to opposing views about Japan. His father was a loyal American, but he was born in Japan and had lived here most of his life. He was married to a Japanese woman and had two children by her. The wellspring of Neil's fortune was in Japan, with tributaries flowing in from other Asian countries. He opposed Japan's rampant imperialism, but his roots penetrated too deeply into Japanese soil to be pulled up like a stray weed and discarded.

"We may have to get out of Japan, Bill, but we'll be back. Maybe not me; I'm too old. But the family will."

With some heat, Bill had replied, "Not me. Maybe I'll look after Macneil interests in the United States. Or, who knows, I might become an airline pilot. Let Ship or Chankoro take care of things in Japan, if the damned Japanese don't confiscate everything we own."

"Ship's too young to think about a career. I can't tell yet what he might become. All he seems to think about now is his mother. And Chankoro? God only knows. If she marries that pianist, no telling where she'll end up. No, it's you, Bill, whom I count on to carry on for me. It has to be you."

"Dammit, Dad, I just don't want anything more to do with the Japanese."

"Do you really hate them so much, Son? Why? What has turned you against them so? I remember those summers when you used to have fistfights with the children of our China branch managers about the Chinese and the Japanese. You always stood up for the Japanese."

"You know very well what happened."

"You mean Nanking."

"Of course."

"But Son, you *can't* let that single outrage dominate the rest of your life."

Finally, Bill Macneil went to his cabin, which was cooler than he expected. Two fans were churning away, one directing its flow toward the single bunk over a large block of ice sitting in a basin. The portholes were open but the curtains had been pulled shut, dimming the cabin's interior and making the furniture ill-defined.

Someone seemed to be asleep under a sheet in his bunk. Could he have gotten into the wrong cabin? Switching on the light, Bill saw with a sinking feeling of resignation that the bunk's occupant was who he had most feared it would be.

"Did you plan to stow away, Helma?" He supposed she had grown sleepy waiting for him.

"If you'll let me, I will," the Swiss girl said, smiling warmly.

Bill pulled a chair next to the bunk, forcing some cordiality into his tone. "Well, I'm glad we have this chance to say goodbye. No telling when we'll have a chance to see each other again."

"I could visit you in America," Helma said, holding the sheet tight against her chin. And thee will be coming back next summer, yes?"

"Helma, listen. My father thinks America will be at war with Japan very soon. In fact, he is trying to transfer everything we own out of Japan just as soon as he can."

Helma's expression sobered, alarm in her eyes.

"If war starts," Bill went on, "it's certain I'll join the army."

"But they won't take thee with that bad ankle," she protested.

"I won't tell them."

"No, no! Thee must not go to war! Oh, no! I could not bear that. Just the thought of thee killing other men, bombing cities, sinking ships."

"If my country goes to war, I'll do my duty. You know that, Helma. We've been over this often enough."

"Brotherly love, Bill! Why can't I persuade thee to see the light? Love thy fellow man, Bill darling. Just say no to the war-mongers." Her tone was desperate.

Macneil stiffened. "It was Japan, Helma, that sent her armies into China and Manchuria. Not my country."

"It's thy country that cut off Japan from the oil and raw materials she needs to survive."

Bill's voice rose in anger. "If you had seen what I saw in Nanking, you would not—"

"I know what happened to thee in Nanking," she said quietly.

"How do you know?"

"Chankoro told me the whole story. I'm terribly sorry about that, but going to war with Japan will not restore thy Ellen. We must show our love through forgiveness. Please, oh, please! Thee must not even think of going to war."

Macneil was alarmed by Helma's frequent use of the word 'thee.' He knew enough about the Friends to know their women used that expression only with men they loved.

He held on to his anger and tried to talk rationally to this woman of such tempting nubility. "Even if I don't go to war myself, dear—" he gritted his teeth on the word 'dear' "—we may not be able to go back and forth between Japan and America for a long while. That's why you and your parents really should leave Japan soon. Return to Switzerland. You'll be safe there."

"Does my safety matter to thee?"

"Of course."

"Why?"

"I . . . I'm fond of you, you know."

"That is all? Does thee not love me . . . a little?"

Bill looked away. "I think I could love thee—I mean, you—Helma, but we only met three months ago and—"

"Thee loved Ellen, did thee not?"

"For God's sake, I was only fifteen when I knew her in Nanking."

"And because of that memory, thee cannot love me?"

"I did not say that."

"I love thee."

Bill reached out to pull down the sheet covering Helma. He wanted to take her hand in his for what he was trying to say, but she pulled the sheet out of his grasp.

"I'm afraid you'll have to go, Helma. This ship will be leaving soon."

A determined look came over her face, turning down the corners of her timeless smile. "How much longer can I stay?"

"I don't know. Maybe an hour. Possibly less."

"That will be time enough," she said, throwing back the sheet. She was totally, gloriously naked, right down to her sparse golden pubic hair.

"My God!" Bill gasped, unable to tear his eyes from her luscious figure with its tight waist, long legs and neck . . . or from the lewd marks she had painted with lipstick on her nipples and nether lips.

In blatant invitation, Helma raised her knees and opened her legs. She was blushing furiously, intensifying the pale blue of her enormous eyes.

"I'm sorry. I had to do this. I want thee to have my virginity as a . . . going-away present. Then I know thee will come back to me."

"Helma, I can't . ."

"Yes, thee can. Quick, lock the door. I've already doubled up a towel and spread it under me. Come closer. I'll undo thy belt. Thee must do this—or I'll die. Can thee not see how much it shames me to do this? I love thee, dearest. Don't make me beg.
"Thee are my only chance for happiness in this life. Oh, darling, come. Take me. . . . take me. . . ."

Exactly forty-seven minutes after five o'clock that afternoon the tug at the bow began to push *City of Glasgow* away from the dock and into the harbor.

A forlorn Helma Graf stood on the dock, her cheeks wet with tears. She waved farewell to Bill Macneil, who responded uncertainly.

He knew he should say more than goodbye—after what had just happened. The distance between them was not yet great. No one else was near at hand, so he took a grip on himself and said in a voice he hoped would carry to her ears, "I—love—you."

Helma's face brightened. She clasped her hands beneath her chin in a prayer gesture. "I hope thee really do."

His voice strengthened. "Go back to Switzerland, Helma. Take your parents with you."

She was thoughtful for a moment but alarmed by the growing distance between them. She cried, "But I can't. God's work is here. I must—"

The freighter's horn obliterated all sounds. By the time it had faded, the distance to the dock had doubled, then tripled.

Helma's lips were still moving but Bill could not make out her words.

As her figure grew smaller, he looked over her head and saw Mount Fuji half obscured by summer mist and the belching smoke from Yokohama's factories.

On clear fall days, the mountain was usually visible in all its pristine beauty. That autumnal, snow-tipped Fuji represented to Bill Macneil the Japan of the past—before 1937 and Nanking. The industrial smoke was Japan's new militarism. Could Helma Graf be part of the past he wanted so much to put behind him?

Her shrinking figure saddened him. He doubted the Swiss girl would ever leave Japan. Her fondness for these complex people was as great as his dislike. He had no intention of returning and was doubtful—with that bone of contention festering between them—that he would ever ask her to join him elsewhere.

CHAPTER 5

Dairen, Manchuria
September 1941

Sarah Macneil wasted little time before calling on her paunchy future father-in-law Joseph Blum. (God, she thought, what chemistry of nature produced a marvel like Nathan from these loins?) Perfunctorily she kissed him on the cheek. "You wanted to see me?"

"Sit, my dear girl." His English was Frenchified but usually understandable. Unlike his son, Joseph had never learned Chinese. Knowing Russian—he was born there and had emigrated to France—French, and English were more than enough for one man, he always explained.

"You told Nathan you would be able to put some of your family money to our little project," he said.

"I hope, sir, it will become more than a 'little project.'" Sarah's voice was a lilting soprano.

"It will, I am sure. Anyway, that's marvelous news."

Sitting demurely beside Joseph Blum's desk, Sarah waited. She knew there would be more.

"I've heard of a job I think you should apply for."

"A job? I have a job, Mr. Blum. It's an easy one and that gives me free time to be with your son. Once we're married, I don't expect to work at all."

"Hear me out, Sarah." Joseph Blum carefully lit one of the Havana cigars he was addicted to. "Colonel Kazuo Ishihara has let it be known he wants to employ a young, attractive, trilingual female assistant. He hasn't found anyone with those qualifications yet."

Sarah straightened up. "I know about Ishihara. In fact, I've met him. He's supposed to be in charge of everything that goes on behind the scenes in the Japanese administration."

"That's right. He's chief of the secret police—but he's also General Doihara's right-hand man. In fact, he has almost as much influence as the general."

"And you think if I were his assistant, I could help promote Far East Zion?"

Joseph Blum nodded energetically. "That's what we have in mind. You're young, attractive—indeed, beautiful, and you speak Chinese, Japanese, and English. The one hitch is that you hold an American passport."

Sarah nodded. After a moment's thought, she said, "I also have a kind of Chinese citizenship. When my grandfather was Japan's ambassador in Peking, his closest Chinese friend was governor of the province. In congratulating Grandfather on my birth in the embassy, he sent along a certificate of Chinese citizenship with a note saying it might be useful to me some day. I didn't know governors could confer citizenship, but in China all things are possible."

"Ishihara might take a Chinese citizen. For obvious reasons, he would not employ an American or Britisher."

Sarah shook her head sadly. "I don't know . . . After we marry, Nathan wants to go to America for more training."

"I know. I'm trying to persuade him to postpone leaving for a year to help me get FEZ on its feet."

"He's very enthusiastic about that."

"Especially now with all the talk about war. Jewish refugees have been streaming out of Europe for several years. They are living temporarily here and there all over the world. They desperately need a place like Manchuria for permanent settlement, with America almost impossible for them to enter."

"But if war starts, won't that interfere with the project?"

"It would, of course, but let's pray actual hostilities won't begin for a year or so at least."

"But if they begin sooner?"

"Then we still have the problem of what to do with the sixteen thousand Jews already in Manchuria. Most of them are living hand to mouth with little prospect of decent jobs and homes. What we need in Manchuria is an industrial base—factories and businesses—where their skills and our capital can be put to good use."

"Nathan has talked of little else since I returned from Tokyo last month. By the way, where is he?"

"Isn't he with you? He didn't come home last night. I thought he . . . he might have spent the night with you."

"Of course not." Nathan had never spent the night in her apartment, and Sarah resented his father's assumption. "He was supposed to call me last night at seven. I waited all evening."

Joseph Blum was silent, but alarm was clear in his eyes.

Two days later, the ransom note reached the trembling hands of Joseph Blum. It was written in Chinese and demanded fifty thousand gold yuan. The packet containing the note also held the little finger of Nathan Blum's left hand, spelling an end to the young man's dreams of ever becoming a concert pianist.

Joseph ran about desperately trying to raise the fifty thousand. Sarah cabled her father to authorize the Dairen branch of the Macneil hong to advance her the thirteen thousand yuan Joseph had been unable to gather.

With the fifty thousand yuan in hand at last, Joseph Blum waited six more days for word from the kidnappers, but none came. He sought the advice of the French vice consul, who cautioned against paying anything without proof the son was still alive.

The second communication came in the form of a telephone call telling Joseph where to leave the sacks of gold coins. Hesitantly, Blum asked for proof his son was alive. The following morning an eight-year-old Chinese girl brought a carefully wrapped index finger to the Blum residence. (A doctor confirmed it had been cut from a living person.) Joseph's keening was heard by the neighbors throughout the day.

Blum determined to deliver the gold as demanded, but reported the ransom call to the French vice consul. At the vice consul's behest the Japanese Kempeitai or secret police and their Chinese myrmidons set a trap.

To everyone's surprise they captured the three Chinese kidnappers. After a night of picturesque torture featuring sophisticated refinements that shocked even Colonel Ishihara, the police learned the whereabouts of Nathan Blum.

They found him in a hole in a field, but the gangrenous

stumps of the pianist's fingers had not been tended, and Nathan was dying from loss of blood and exposure. (Manchurian nights in October can be severe.) An ambulance rushed him to the Sisters of Mercy Hospital near the center of Dairen. When Sarah arrived, she found Joseph Blum incoherent in his grief, his body racked by sobs and shudders.

Sarah's eyes blazed with rage when she heard the doctor's despairing words. Only five foot two, Sarah appeared taller as she strode stiffly erect into Nathan's room. There was a fiercely protective manner about her as she sharply motioned the others away from the bedside of her moribund fiancé.

She had come just in time.

"Darling, I—"

"Be quiet and listen, Sarah," Nathan whispered. "I haven't the strength for . . . for more than a few words. Do you love me?"

Sarah Macneil nodded grimly.

"Then hear my last wish. It's about . . . FEZ." Nathan's voice dropped even lower. Spittle appeared at the corner of his mouth. "Sarah . . . please . . . help our Jews . . . Promise me you will . . . get them to safety. . . . somewhere. . . ."

"I promise, Nathan. I promise."

"Very . . . well. Carry on, Sergeant . . . Macneil."

That was one of their private jokes. He was the captain, she the sergeant in their comedy routines.

"Yes, my captain. You . . . you carry on, too . . ." Sarah choked on her words.

There was a final gurgle. Nathan Blum seemed to shrink within himself.

He had departed for another Zion.

For a long time Sarah slumped motionless beside Nathan's

bed. In her imagination Nathan sat at a piano on the stage of a concert hall in Paris. Before an elite audience he was playing a program of tuneful, sensual music. His ten slim fingers had a graceful touch and he played the music with a lilt.

For an encore, he played—after a bow to Sarah Macneil in the audience—one of her favorites, "La Paloma."

"Well done, my love," Sarah whispered to herself. "Without all ten fingers you had no use for this old body anyway. Now carry on, my captain, to more glittering triumphs. I know you will dazzle the celestial audiences. Oh, God," she sobbed, "can I possibly live without him?"

Joseph Blum went mad with grief. His widow sold the Blum holdings in Manchuria, and the couple disappeared into oblivion.

Vowing to honor her promise to the dying Nathan Blum, Sarah "Chankoro" Macneil entered the employ of Colonel Kazuo Ishihara of the Japanese secret police. The colonel was satisfied with her certificate of Chinese citizenship.

He was also greatly impressed by her statement that she was a granddaughter of ex-Ambassador Tomoji Miyoshi, a senior advisor to the Ministry of Foreign Affairs in Tokyo.

CHAPTER 6

Tokyo, Japan
October 1941

About the time of Nathan Blum's death, a short, rumpled Japanese man limped out of an apartment near the entrance to the Meiji Shrine in Tokyo. He climbed awkwardly into the rear of a car-for-hire.

The apartment belonged to the man's mistress; the car was paid for by the Rikken Laboratory in western Tokyo. Both the woman and the car had been made possible by the man's recent appointment as head of the nuclear physics division of Rikken. Known as the "Father of the New Physics" in Japan, he had built his country's first cyclotron—a 26-incher. His next project was construction of a gigantic 60-incher weighing 220 tons.

At barely five feet, Chinda Nishikawa was sometimes mistaken for a dwarf. His withered left arm was deformed at birth, and he dragged his left foot when he walked. As happens, the strength that should have gone into his arm and foot went into his mind.

He was a true genius with a doctorate in electrical engineering from the Imperial University in Tokyo. He had studied at Cambridge under Ernest Rutherford, a Nobel Prize laureate, and at Niels Bohr's Institute of Theoretical Physics in Copenhagen. He had become an expert in cosmic rays and quantum mechanics.

In 1940 and 1941 Nishikawa had published four well-received papers on fission experimentation. One was entitled "Induced (Beta) Activity of Uranium by Fast Neutrons," prompting a leading American scientist, Arthur H. Compton, to postulate that Japan's work in atomic research was at about the same advanced stage of development as America's'.

Doctor Nishikawa had discovered a new uranium isotope, U-237, which was the same chemically as U-238 but different atomically.

That cool fall morning the hire-car transported the distinguished gnome of an atomic scientist to his office in the Rikken Laboratory, a mammoth complex of 54 buildings erected in 1917.

On his desk Nishikawa found notification that the anxiously awaited research grant from the Japanese air force had reached Rikken's accounting section. If Doctor Nishikawa had been demonstrative, and physically able, he would have leaped onto his desk and danced a jig. With this money he could move ahead rapidly with several projects. One of them was a nuclear weapon—a bomb—for the air force.

The Japanese navy also wanted to give him money to develop nuclear weapons for them. Fine. He would take their money, too. The more the better. He had more ideas than they had money.

Sadly, Dr. Chinda Nishikawa was an unpleasant man. He was terse, rude, inconsiderate, and arrogant. His new mistress did not like him at all and regretted she had entered into their patron-protégée arrangement. His wife was thankful her husband had a mistress, since it meant he would seldom be home to torment her and their two children, who feared him as if he were an ogre from a Japanese folk tale.

CHAPTER 7

San Francisco, California
March 1942

Events seemed to come in clusters.

For months an uneasy Bill Macneil had bided his time. At last, more was to happen in one day than during the three months since that date in December 1941 that would "live in infamy."

He strode toward his off-campus apartment, breathing deeply the morning air of another fine San Francisco day. The morning mists were being defeated by the warming sun. He had finished his two early classes and had nothing to do except study until his three o'clock.

Since it was Friday, he wondered if he should fly up to the Mount Shasta area for more training with his mountain rescue team or stay home and study for mid-terms. If he stayed, he might go to Chinatown tomorrow for Shanghai cuisine. An added attraction would be the lovely waitress of Chinese extraction who often favored him with languid looks from her dark, almond-shaped eyes. Unconsciously, Bill quickened his steps and took a sharp breath.

A block from campus he passed two young men in obviously new army uniforms. One of them had sat near him in a physics class last semester.

"Hey, Macneil. You signed up yet?"

"Not yet."

"Better hurry. War will be over."

Bill didn't argue. He walked on, knowing the war would be hard and long. He would like to have seen Japan beaten to her knees and ground into the earth immediately, but he knew the Japanese too well. They would put up a stubborn resistance.

Bill knew the Japanese were capable of acts both puzzling and contradictory, even to him. Only last week, for instance, he had read that shortly after sinking *HMS Prince of Wales* and *Repulse* off the coast of Malaya, pilots of the Japanese naval air force had flown low over the site of the sinkings and dropped bouquets of flowers on the ships' watery graves. "Because," the pilots later explained, "the British warships died such beautiful deaths." An amazing people.

That event did nothing to diminish Bill's hatred of his former neighbors for what they had done at Nanking, but it did warn him that if he was to fight against them in the Pacific, he might face other danger-laden unpredictabilities.

Taking two letters from his mailbox, he glanced at the return addresses, then mounted the three flights in a burst of energy.

Inside his two-room apartment, he stroked his black cat Satan and hurriedly gave him a saucer of milk. Flinging his jacket over a chair, he flopped onto the sofa and hungrily tore open the letter from his father. He had gone no farther than the date and "Dear Son," when the doorbell rang.

With an impatient grunt, he opened the door to find an army captain in full uniform. His lapel insignia was a sphinx, with which Macneil was unfamiliar.

"Bill Macneil? I'm David Spencer. I'd like to talk to you."

Stuffing his father's letter in his pocket, Bill gestured for the officer to enter, wondering what business the army had with him, although they would have a grip on him soon enough.

Captain Spencer was dark and almost as tall as Macneil. He was lean and seemed fit. He had prominent teeth, oversize ears, and a mobile mouth under a trim moustache.

"I saw you looking at my insignia," he said, taking a straight chair. "Not many people know it. It's military intelligence. Have you read your mail yet? The letters are from your father and Helma Graf."

"What the devil! Did you read my mail? You have no damned right to—" Bill was furious.

"Simmer down, Macneil. We're at war. We can do a lot more if we choose to. I *didn't* read your letters, but I suggest you go ahead and glance through the one from your father. I know you've been waiting for it, and we can probably have a more productive chat after you've seen what he has to say."

His eyes still hot with resentment, Macneil removed his father's letter from his pocket and ignored the army captain for the moment.

> Dear Bill,
>
> I am aboard a Swedish repatriation vessel scheduled to dock in Goa within the hour. I would like to mail this letter here and so haven't much time.
>
> The Japanese attacked Pearl Harbor

before even I thought they would. All our assets were frozen, but I managed to transfer most of our movable holdings out of Japan before then.

I was holding space for Umeko, Shipton, and myself on this ship but in the last week before sailing, Umeko came down with uremic poisoning occasioned by kidney failure. It's her diabetes, of course. The doctors absolutely forbade that she be moved. She's in the Seventh Day Adventist hospital in Shinjuku, in good hands.

Shipton insisted on staying with her. He has a stout heart, that boy, at least as far as his mother is concerned. Since she is a Japanese national and he is a minor (although holding an American passport), his status presents no problem . . . yet. The Japanese were understanding about that. Shipton is fifteen, and if he has to remain in Japan until he turns eighteen, he will become an *adult* enemy alien—and that *will* be a problem.

Anyway, I hope I will be able to change ships in Goa to a vessel bound for a South American port and from there

make my way back to the USA. Upon
arrival, I will go to SF first to see you if
you're not already in uniform.
Much love from,
Dad

P.S. Your sweetheart (?) Helma Graf's
parents are on this vessel. Good people, I
think. Helma stayed on in Japan.
She is a Swiss and neutral and, of
course, in a different category from
us in the view of the Japanese. Still,
things won't be easy for her. The
Japanese will probably mistake her
for an American. She was talking
about making an arm-band identifying
her as Swiss. She did us a big favor,
though, by moving into our house in
Azabu . . . at my invitation.
That permitted us to nail a sign
on the gate saying this was the
residence of a citizen of a neutral
country. Of course, Umeko retains her
Japanese citizenship and Shipton
is a minor. I left a sizable amount
in a bank account in Umeko's name,
but when I heard from one of our
bankers that Japan planned to
limit the amount of cash that could
be withdrawn from ordinary accounts

even by Japanese, I took out the
equivalent of $60,000 and hid it in
three caches in the house, one
known only to Umeko, one to Shipton,
and one to Helma.
(I think you can imagine why.)

Bill Macneil felt the tension of recent months drain from his body. Except for his sister, Chankoro, he now knew what had become of his family. Slowly, he turned to the army captain. Remembering his manners, Bill offered him a drink, which was accepted. Bill was somewhat suspicious of this sharp-toned man who seemed to be watching his mail, but this was no time to be influenced by minor animosities.

"Well, David, how can I help you?" Bill asked, calling the captain by his given name. He had not the least intention of kow-towing to military rank . . . yet. Besides, the man was hardly older than Bill, if at all.

Captain Spencer nodded his head toward a wall plaque. "Member—Mt. Shasta Rescue Team." He sipped his anchor steam beer. "Been called out lately?"

"Not since early January. That what you came to talk about?"

David Spencer laughed. "Not by any means, but your experience as a parachutist could be of considerable interest to us."

Bill wondered at the man's use of "us." "You know someone who needs rescuing?"

Abruptly, David Spencer began speaking to his host in Japanese. To Bill's utter amazement, the army officer's Japanese was impeccable—really of native quality. Macneil's surprise must have shown on his face.

Continuing in Japanese, Spencer said, "Do I surprise you?"
Replying in Japanese, Bill said, "There aren't many of us. How
did you learn?"

"Born to missionary parents in rural Shikoku. Only way I
could get myself educated was to go through the Japanese school
system. I must say you're pretty good yourself. I had heard you
were the best, but I wanted to make sure. How about the written
language?"

Bill grinned. "Want to give me a test?"

"We'll get around to that. What I wanted to do today was ask
you about your plans. Won't you be finishing your third year in
college soon?"

"To tell you the truth, I was waiting to hear about my family. I wanted to stay flexible in case they needed me—somewhere."

"What did your father write?"

"You mean you really don't know? Well, here. Go ahead. I
assume you could have found out, anyway."

Quickly, Spencer glanced through the letter. "Do you plan on
volunteering for service this year?"

"Probably."

"Then we have a proposal for you."

"We?"

"Military intelligence. We would like for you to stay right
where you are. I'll get you a deferment if they try to draft you.
When we're ready, we'll have you come to Washington, where we
will commission you. Same rank as me. Then it's off to paratroop
school."

"I don't need to go to school to learn how to—"

"There's a military way to drop from aircraft and a civilian
way, Bill. We want you to do it the military way."

"And then?"

"You'll lead a team of translators and interpreters in the Pacific."

Macneil bridled. "Why go to paratroop school to sit at a desk and translate documents? That's not how I want to fight the god-damned Japanese."

"We're forming a unit called ATIS—Allied Translator and Interpreter Service. Some of its members will be 'combat interrogation officers.' Their job will be to parachute behind Japanese lines, capture prisoners, and interrogate them on the spot. They may even have to kill the prisoners after interrogation, to preserve the team's safety." Spencer laughed. "How does that strike you? Derring-do enough?"

"What do I do till you call me?"

"Stay where you are. Our country is desperate for men who can translate and interpret, so we've set up a Japanese language school in the Presidio. I'm one of the recruiters. Let me tell you, Bill, it's not an easy job. All the Japanese Americans on the coast are being sent to relocation camps inland, and white Americans who claim to know Japanese are damned few and hard to locate. Most of those I've found don't handle Japanese well enough for the work we have in mind. Some of them speak kitchen Japanese but could never translate a military document. That's why we will have to send them to school for a year or so. Which is where you come in. We would like to send you some of these prospective students and ask you to judge their abilities. Interview them in Japanese. Ask them to read and translate a Japanese newspaper. See if they can decipher a letter in grass-writing—because that's how some of the diaries we pick up on the battlefield will be written."

Spencer paused. "How about it?"

"I like that part about dropping behind enemy lines."

"One more thing. We've been told how much you hate the Japanese. That's all right, because we're all supposed to hate them now. Only thing is, if your hatred is too excessive, that may interfere with your ability to interrogate POWs. The manual says we can extract more intelligence from a POW if we can establish some sort of rapport. Not friendship, of course, no one expects that. But if your hatred shines through too strongly, the POW will clam up, become surly, and refuse to say anything."

Macneil was silent for a long moment. "I hate them all right—for something they did in Nanking—"

"We know about that."

"But I was born in Japan and there was a time when I had more Japanese friends than American. Hell, my stepmother is Japanese. My brother and sister are half-Japanese. I guess I could conceal my dislike enough to do interrogations."

"By the way, where is your sister Sarah?"

"I wish I knew. She was in Dairen, Manchuria, the last I heard."

"Another branch of our service might want to talk to you about her some day."

After Spencer left, Bill Macneil reread his father's letter, then opened the one from Helma Graf—after some thoughtful hesitation.

It was the first time he had heard directly from Helma since waving goodbye in Yokohama. Her silence had been a relief, in a way, because he feared that complications would arise from what he had regarded as a passing affair. But then, by the end of 1941, he began to feel some concern for her. Gradually, his thoughts about Helma became more positive. He recalled her persistent pursuit of the man—himself—she professed to love to the point of distraction: What had been a bother was taking on a certain charm. He found himself admiring her retention of chastity until she felt obligated to sacrifice it in a last-gasp effort to tighten her hold on the target of her devotion.

Even her annoying use of the juvenile expression 'jeepers' seemed cuter than it did obnoxious. He remembered more fondly what he could only describe as her looks of desperate innocence.

On those nights he slept alone, his last waking thoughts were more often of Helma than the Chinese waitress on Grant Street or that sophisticated, high-toned, eager young lady from Nob Hill. The memory of Helma's naked body in his cabin on the *City of Glasgow* shone through the mists of encroaching slumber with remarkable clarity. Her lewd lipstick decorations on her intimate parts repelled him less and fascinated him more. What had been a confused, hurried, and startingly abrupt coupling took on—seven months later—the more engaging aspect of a rhapsodic adventure in sweet lust.

He found himself longing for an opportunity to repeat the experience.

Even so, his changing perception of Helma did not extend to marrying this strange, determined female who steadfastly refused to see evil in the hearts of men who actually had not a scintilla of good anywhere within them.

Helma's letter was disappointingly brief. Even though she addressed him as "My dearest Bill" and employed "thee" and "thou" liberally, her letter made him wonder if someone was reading it over her shoulder—or if she thought someone would later invade the privacy of her mail.

She was sorry, she wrote, that she had been so remiss in her correspondence. One reason was that most Westerners still in Japan were sending their foreign mail out through the International Red Cross, but many voiced suspicions that Japan's secret police—both the *Tokko Keisatsu* (Special Political Police) and the Kempeitai—were censoring letters.

Helma had waited until she could make an arrangement with a family friend in the Swiss Embassy to send out her messages in the diplomatic pouch for delivery to Pepin and Lurlei Schwerz in Zug, Switzerland. Pepin was her father's first cousin. She had written instructing him how to handle her communications. Even getting nonofficial letters from Switzerland to the United States in wartime was time-consuming—but not impossible.

He could, she wrote, send letters to her—if he had not forgotten her—by the same route in reverse, and she included Pepin and Lurlei's mailing address in Zug.

Helma's letter was written in January, before the Swedish repatriation vessel *Gripsholm* sailed the following month, but Helma believed her parents would be aboard. She was thinking about moving into Bill's Tokyo home to be of whatever assistance she could to his family. Also, it would benefit her in that she would no longer have to travel back and forth between Tokyo and her parents' home in far-off Shizuoka Prefecture.

Before Bill could wonder why she would not stay in Shizuoka—a better place than Tokyo to take shelter from the uncertain dangers of war—Helma sprang her surprise. "I am thinking about taking a job. Missionary work seems out of the question. Although I am a Swiss neutral and legally free to move about Japan even as the Japanese can move about my country, it doesn't work that way in actuality. Too many people assume I am American or English and therefore cause problems. This inconveniences the Germans, too, even though they are allies of the Japanese. Anyway, what work would I do? I am not sure. I might obtain a clerical position at the Swiss Embassy. I have also heard Radio Tokyo may be hiring persons fluent in English. Anyway, I must have money for living expenses, so we will see. I love thee. Helma."

CHAPTER 8

Shanghai, China
October 1942

Sarah "Chankoro" Macneil was living in a comfortable but small apartment in the International Settlement of Shanghai.

She lived alone, although Colonel Kazuo Ishihara was a frequent visitor, occasionally staying all night.

Her Chinese amah-san, Mrs. Chang, had basement quarters and came every day. Sarah's job was special assistant to Ishihara, who had been transferred to staff duty under Major General Kenji Doihara, commander-in-chief of the Imperial Japanese Army for the Shanghai area. Besides his other duties, Ishihara was in charge of the 16,000 Jewish refugees in Shanghai.

The largest assembly area for the Jews was Pootung Civil Assembly Center. The Pootung Jews were stateless refugees or were carrying passports of enemy nations: America, Great Britain, and others. Jews with Russian or Iraqi passports, for example, were still free to move about Shanghai. All the Manchurian Jews had been brought to Pootung.

About 3,000 of the Jews had been German, but many of these had left their homeland without proper documents and the rest did not want to identify themselves as German, fearing what might be done to them by an ally of the Nazis. They sought safety in statelessness.

Germany's "final solution" to the Jewish question had begun in January 1942. Japan was well aware how "final" the German "solution" was. For all their resentment of the West, the Japanese were not prepared to go as far as the Germans.

The Blums' Far East Zion plan came apart late the previous year, right after Pearl Harbor. War obviated any hope that American Jews, under the guidance of Rabbi Stephen Wise—who soon condemned any Jew who supported Japan's aims—would invest in an industrial base in Manchuria to nurture Wise's coreligionists. Nor would the Japanese, with all-out war confronting them in the Pacific, consider the expending of their own resources to establish a prosperous and stable alien population there.

Japanese who had favored the Blums' FEZ concept—including Colonel Ishihara and, to a lesser extent, General Doihara—were ordered to halt all such grandiose machinations as FEZ and to assemble forthwith the refugee Jews then in Manchuria and move them to a central camp in occupied China where they could be watched. Refurbishing the Pootung barracks and the mass movement had taken seven months.

Sarah was pleased the Pootung buildings had roofs, the water supply was adequate, and garbage was collected. Sewage facilities, however, were primitive, medicines were in short supply, and the inhabitants would soon, she thought, begin to show signs of malnutrition as the supplies of food they had brought with them began to run out. There were already a few cases of beriberi,

malaria, dysentery, and some heart infections.

Sarah's problem was how to do as much as she could for the Jews in obedience to her vow to the dying Nathan Blum, without arousing the suspicions of Colonel Ishihara.

Kazuo Ishihara was actually a decent man, although Sarah's true feelings toward him were not anything at all like those she pretended. He had a wife and family at home in Fukuoka, Japan, and was twenty-one years older than she. Fanatically clean, he wore glasses and a trim moustache and was an inch shorter than Sarah, who was herself quite short. How he performed as a lover, Sarah was not qualified to judge since she had little basis for comparison. To be sure, Ishihara was hardly the equal of Nathan Blum, but Sarah could not believe anyone could equal him in any way.

As Ishihara's Girl Friday, Sarah Macneil—who went by Lin Hsiao-mai—had been given numerous administrative assignments involving the Pootung Center. Ishihara seemed satisfied with her work and was gradually giving her more responsibility. How much of that trust derived from her work and how much from his sexual satisfaction, Sarah could not say. Probably both.

Kazuo Ishihara was no anti-Semite. In fact, he had come to regard himself as a kind of guardian of the Pootung Jews. With Sarah's encouragement, he had done much for them, although the Jews voiced acrid complaints about their treatment at the hands of the Japanese administrators.

Jewish complaints Ishihara could handle. His real problems came on one hand from Colonel Gerhardt Kahner, the recently arrived Gestapo chief for the Shanghai area. At Kahner's first interview with Ishihara, the German had wasted no time coming directly and bluntly to the point.

"My mission here, Colonel Ishihara, is to urge you to let us help you with a solution to the Jewish problem in Shanghai."

Since the two colonels had no language in common, Sarah was present to interpret the German's English and Ishihara's Japanese.

An unconscious grimace appeared on Ishihara's face. "I have heard of your 'solution' to the problem of the Jews."

Kahner pressed on eagerly. "Then I am certain you can see how much assistance we can offer you, what with our broad experience in these matters."

"I don't think we have quite come to that yet, Colonel Kahner. And whatever solution—as you call it—we arrive at will, I am sure, be a purely Japanese solution. We have our ways, Colonel, and you have yours. I fear we will seldom find them in harmony with each other."

Kahner's face—with a *Schmiss* or dueling scar—mottled with suppressed anger. "We were led to understand by your ambassador in Berlin that we would be accorded an advisory role in this matter."

"Tell me, just why is this a matter of such concern to the Third Reich? We are, after all, thousands of miles from Germany. There are no German forces in the Far East and very few of your nationals. For my own curiosity, I would like to know why a pocket of Jews here in Shanghai is of so much concern to you."

Kahner sputtered, "For one thing, many of your Jews have—or had—German nationality, even though they won't admit it."

"Would you like to send them back to Germany? I believe we have about three thousand German Jews. How do you propose to transport them? Overland? Across Mongolia and through Russia? By sea? You would have to fill several passenger liners and move

them around the Cape of Good Hope and finally through the English Channel. And who would pay for all this, Colonel Kahner? I can assure you, even without referring the question to General Doihara, my country will not."

Kahner rose with a curse in German. "Does your country intend to coddle these vermin?"

"I will gladly allow you to spend a week in one of the Pootung barracks, Colonel. Then you can tell me if we are coddling them."

"Don't be ridiculous." Kahner spun around and snarled over his shoulder, "We will see about this." The thud of his boots was the only sound of his departure.

Ishihara smiled at Sarah. "We haven't seen the last of him, I'm afraid."

Ishihara's second difficulty was with his superior, General Doihara, which did not concern the Pootung Jews since the general was content to entrust their affairs to his subordinate. It was, rather, Ishihara's girl Friday in whom Doihara was more keenly interested.

Coming from behind his desk, the diminutive colonel sat beside Sarah and took one of her hands in his. The office door was closed, so no one dared enter without invitation.

Ishihara spoke in Japanese. "Has the general made any more overtures to you? I must know. To speak the truth, I lose much sleep over you. I don't want to give you up, but I'm afraid if I don't, he will ruin my career. Has he said anything? Have you given him any encouragement?" There was a puppy-like pleading in the colonel's desperate eyes. Of course, as a Japanese man, he would never say he was desperately in love with her, although those words would do more to bind Sarah to him than any others.

"Nothing has happened since that meeting I told you about three weeks ago." Actually, that was not the truth. More had happened, but Sarah was not going to tell her patron about it. She was playing a dangerous game. There might well come a time—and not too far off, at that—when the general could do more, given his rank, to save her Jews than the colonel. She refused to ignore any possibility to save them.

Ishihara was still an officer of the Special Political Police—*Tokko Keisatsu*—although on detached duty with Doihara's staff. He maintained relations with the agents he had recruited in Manchuria. If he ever learned of Sarah's secret rendezvous with General Doihara, she was uncertain how far Doihara's protection of her would extend.

Nevertheless, that was a chance she was determined to take. Even now the Pootung Jews were in desperate straits. How much worse would their situation become if Tokyo decided to let the Gestapo take a hand in the administration of Pootung was a nightmarish possibility that terrified Sarah.

She thought of herself as the *Kakure Tenshi*—the Hidden Angel—of the Pootung Jews and wanted to keep all the allies she could enlist.

CHAPTER 9

Tokyo, Japan
December 1942

The first year of the war had not yet brought serious inconveniences for Tokyo residents.

To be sure, the Japanese living standard had always been low. Privation had grown throughout the 1930s as Japan's imperialist war in China siphoned resources. In this last month of 1942, few Japanese could have dreamed what lay in store for them—and in the near future. The Doolittle air raid on Tokyo in April might have served as a wake-up for a few, but the harm done to the capital was a mosquito's teardrop, as the Japanese would say, to what would befall them over the next two and a half years.

That morning, Helma Graf, now twenty-two, donned warmer clothing than usual. Although a clear day—Mount Fuji could be distantly seen from the second floor of the Macneil residence in Azabu—it was cold as chill winds from the Siberian landmass swept through the passes of the Japan Alps and over the

Kanto Plain. The young Swiss woman had been sleeping in Bill Macneil's old room. When she pulled the covers over her shoulders at night and composed herself for sleep—after her prayers for universal peace, of course—she never forgot she was comfortably snug in her true love's bed. Blushing hotly in the dark, she wished he were there to comfort and guide her.

She wrote to Bill as often as she dared, but did not want to endanger her channel of communication through the Swiss Embassy. Without any letters from him in return, she could not know if he had received hers. She could only pray he had. She shuddered at the thought that he—having heard nothing from her—had assumed she had forsaken him.

She wished she were as pure as the snow the Tokyo Meteorological Bureau predicted would soon fall. Sadly, she was not. Her seduction of Bill Macneil aboard the *City of Glasgow* shamed her, but the memory of that brief embrace caused her to squeeze her legs together tightly as a mysterious dampness moistened her upper thighs. Nor was she above employing her fingers to encourage the vaginal dew. This embarrassed her even more, but she was powerless against the emotions that flooded through her like a sea-surge when a hurricane buffets a tropical coast.

Helma looked in on Umeko Macneil before leaving. Neil Macneil's wife stayed in bed most of the time, although she had recovered from the uremic poisoning that prevented her from leaving Japan with her husband.

Shipton Macneil had already left for Hiro Senior High School.

Wrapping the band identifying her as a Swiss national around her left arm, Helma walked out of the house toward the nearby Arisugawa Park stop on the trolley line. With one transfer, it would carry her to Radio Tokyo in the Kudan district on the far side of the Imperial Palace. Her clothing was modest, nondescript in color. Her shoes had medium heels. Her blond hair was cut short and mostly hidden under a hat pulled far down on her head. Although obviously foreign, she did not stand out as painfully in a crowd as she might.

At the streetcar stop was a crowd of twenty or so commuters, most of whom Helma recognized. Several smiled hesitantly at her, but a few frowned. Most retained their bland countenances. They seemed complacent, if not content. There were no fat persons among them. In Japan, Helma had learned, the overweight usually rode in chauffeur-driven automobiles.

Her streetcar—Number 11—came and she climbed aboard, showing her commutation ticket. She found a seat, having competed successfully with a healthy-looking young man to reach it first. No Japanese man would relinquish his seat to a woman, even if she were crippled and gasping for breath. Helma recalled her school days at Bryn Mawr College near Philadelphia. There, too, she had ridden streetcars to her classes. Perhaps, the Quaker ambience of brotherly love was why she never lacked for a seat.

Still, she did not allow the constant discourtesy of Japanese men to discourage her from her self-assigned mission. After all, she reminded herself, we are all God's creatures. If we have direct access to God, as the Society of Friends held, then God must have direct access to us, and one day, He would enter into the souls of these benighted ones and open their eyes with a soul-shaking epiphany.

At the Hibiya intersection, Helma transferred to a car bound for Kudan. At Hibiya she was only two short blocks from her favorite place—aside from Bill Macneil's bed—in all Tokyo: the

Florida nightclub. How often she had longed to go there, to sway and turn to the magic of the Argentine tango.

In a mood of desperation, she had determined to teach Shipton Macneil how to tango. She had shoved aside chairs and a table and made enough space in the dining room. There was a phonograph in Sarah's old room, and Helma commandeered it. Ship was willing. At sixteen he was taller than Helma and even shaved now and then. (He claimed to shave every other day, but she did not believe him.) Even Umeko managed to descend the stairs and watch and applaud as they twisted and glided back and forth.

The only problem was that the youngest Macneil had begun to press too close at inappropriate moments with a look in his eyes that unsettled Helma.

Another cause of concern about Ship was that he was becoming more outspoken in his support of the United States in the present conflict. He held an American passport and his brother was extremely anti-Japanese, so that was to be expected, but after all, they were living in Japan, and Ship—unlike his brother Bill—was half-Japanese.

Ship had waxed half-deliriously with rapture when the Doolittle planes flew low over Tokyo in April. He had rushed into the garden and, jumping about, had waved a small American flag at one of the bombers.

Later, Helma scolded him. "You mustn't ever do anything like that again."

He was sullen. "Why not? I'm an American, aren't I? Why shouldn't I cheer for them?"

Helma took his hand. "If word gets around, Ship dear, the *Tokko Keisatsu* will be on our doorstep the next day. You would cause serious trouble for your mother." Helma knew Umeko's welfare was always uppermost to Ship Macneil.

Helma looked out the window of the swaying, rattling street-car. Her stop was close at hand. She had an early appointment to see Captain Horace Milmay, a British turncoat who had found a niche of safety in the war by transferring his allegiance from the British monarchy to the Japanese emperor.

She had gone to work at Radio Tokyo in April, first as a clerk-typist and later as a broadcaster. Now she was the POW specialist at the station and she had a one-hour program on Saturday nights. Other women—all Nisei—broadcast on different topics on other nights. All the programs were called the "Zero Hour." The number of Allied prisoners-of-war in Japan was mounting as the conflict in the South Pacific grew more savage. Helma's job was to relay information about these POWs to their former comrades in the combat zones and, through their comrades, to relatives back home: "Hi, there, you guys. Jeepers, is it ever cold here in Tokyo! First, I've got news about one of your buddies. Private Tom Maxwell is alive and healthy and sends regards to his friends in the Second Marine Division on Guadalcanal. He is doing productive work in a coal mine—never mind exactly where—in Japan. I can tell you he's a lot better off than you fellows are, so why don't you pick up one of our surrender leaflets and raise both hands over your head? Then, just walk on over to the Japanese lines and all that pain and fear and filth will be behind you. God did not mean for men to kill each other, so why are you fighting?"

Helma Graf felt no qualms of conscience about making these broadcasts to Allied military personnel in the South Pacific. Why should she? She was, first of all, Swiss, and that had always meant being neutral. She hated no race or nationality, but loved one and all. Besides, what was wrong about her appeals? She was asking them—the Allies—to lay down their arms and surrender—surrender to the concept of Brotherly Love. Given the same chance she would have said as much to Japanese soldiery. "Quit fighting. For the love of God, stop killing each other! Embrace your enemy."

There had been times when Captain Milmay had tried to change her script to include inflammatory admonitions she thought would only increase the slaughter. So far Helma had resisted his editing, and Baron Matsui had ruled in her favor. She was, after all, Swiss—protected by a treaty of neutrality between Japan and Switzerland. Most of the other broadcasters had dual nationality, so Japan had a whip to crack over their heads.

However, Helma was clear-minded enough to recognize that what made her case somewhat different was that she loved—to the verge of distraction—a man who, as an American, was an enemy of the Japanese and who might even now, for all she knew, be fighting and killing Japanese in Guadalcanal or New Guinea. In rebuttal she riposted to her imaginary prosecutor that she could just as easily have fallen in love with a Japanese. Really? the prosecutor asked. Who, for example? Well, I don't know exactly, just someone—I doubt it, her opponent said. If so, give me a name. All right, I will, Helma answered. Uh—Baron Matsui. Matsui? Yes, Baron Matsui: he's fine-looking, he graduated from Cambridge, and he dances the tango.

If Helma had not given her heart and her chastity to Bill Macneil, she would almost certainly have said yes to Matsui's invitations to go dancing, but now that was out of the question. Or was it? She wondered.

One man who would never engage her affections was

Captain Horace Milmay, whom she faced in the small conference room on the third floor of the Radio Tokyo Building.

Milmay was a sandy-haired Englishman in his early thirties. He had been a radio broadcaster in Hong Kong, with a commission as a reserve officer. When war broke out, he was called to the colors, but the British forces in Hong Kong, including Captain Milmay, surrendered to the Japanese in short order.

Baron Matsui, chief of the foreign broadcast division of Radio Tokyo, had sifted through POW records and had found five Americans and Britishers with broadcasting experience. They were brought to Tokyo for interviews with Matsui.

Of the five, two were rejected out of hand by Matsui. The remaining three were offered the opportunity to make broadcasts in English to Allied forces throughout the Pacific. Only one— Horace Milmay—accepted the offer enthusiastically. The second was doubtful, the third said no unequivocally.

Milmay, out of uniform but with the equivalent yen salary of a captain, was designated an assistant to Baron Matsui. His job was supervising the preparation of the broadcasts, approving script contents, planning broadcasts, and teaching correct delivery to the broadcasters.

At first, Baron Matsui, who came as close to being a British aristocrat as a Japanese could, got along famously with Milmay. They drank and dined together in out-of-the-way corners of the capital, but gradually certain flaws in Milmay's character became apparent to the baron, who began to distance himself from the British officer in mufti. Now Matsui kept a close watch on Milmay, but had yet to find little to complain of in the man's performance of his duties.

If anything, Milmay was leaning too heavily toward the cause of ultranationalistic Japan: the Greater East Asian Co-Prosperity Sphere. His anti-British and anti-American bias was becoming too blatant, too rabid, and the broadcasters themselves—who were given some discretion over the words they spoke over the airwaves—were trying to tone down Milmay's excesses. Matsui, too, recognized that a certain degree of subtlety in these propaganda programs would be more effective than strident, Hitlerian bashing of the Allied broadcasts.

"You don't like me, do you, Helma?" Milmay began.

"I don't really know you, I'm afraid."

"You could get to know me if you wanted to," the British officer said in his precisely enunciated English. "It would be difficult for a couple like ourselves to move about freely in Tokyo these days, but we could meet at your place or in my room, you know."

"I'll bear that in mind, Captain. What did you want to see me about?"

"I have a script here for your next broadcast. I want you to read it over and then discuss it with me."

"I hope it's not like the one you gave me last week."

"Just look it over, Helma. Then we'll talk."

"Very well, Captain."

"And I wish you wouldn't call me 'Captain.' You will notice I'm not wearing a uniform."

"I would hardly expect you to do so—not in war-time Tokyo."

"Is that what you don't like about me—the fact that as a British officer I am now in the employ of the Japanese?"

Helma said nothing, but looked steadily at Milmay. What I really don't like about him, she thought, is that his pale eyes are too close together. Although he was tall and slim and his other features were patrician, the positioning of his eyes made him look crafty. Besides, his voice was pitched too high and dripped with upper-class British condescension.

"After all," he pressed on, "every week you yourself urge the British and the Americans throughout the Pacific theater to surrender. That's all I did, isn't it?" Milmay tried—largely in vain—to inject a degree of warmth into his voice. "So let's do try to be more chummy, what? I'd like that, really I would."

Helma's reply was as frosty as the snowflakes beginning to fall outside Milmay's window. "If that is all, sir, I'll excuse myself."

chapter 10

Washington, D.C.
July 1943

Japanese forces evacuated Guadalcanal in January, and in June the
Allies landed on New Guinea.

Bill Macneil received orders to report for active duty early in
July. Using a voucher authorizing travel to Washington, D.C., he
crossed the country by train. In the capital he found a place to
stay for the night, then telephoned a college friend whose home
was in Washington.

Together, the pair made the rounds of three parties, where
Bill's striking features: aquamarine blue eyes, height, and inim-
itable loose-limbed stride made him a standout among the guests.
His civilian clothing, however, occasioned questioning looks, for
this was a town where young men were making haste to don a
uniform of one color or another. Washington was a mecca for
those with "political influence," and many had found what they
sought: respect for the uniform, safety behind a desk, and a good

time in the evenings.

Bill Macneil had few illusions about what life would be like in a combat zone in the Pacific, but he would prefer that to what Washington had to offer. The artificiality and false camaraderie of cocktail parties and high society held no appeal for him.

The next morning, shortly after eight and with the temperature already steaming, Bill found a taxi that took him to one of the so-called K Buildings that had been hastily constructed along the Mall. Military intelligence had its temporary headquarters there while awaiting completion of the Pentagon that was scheduled for September.

Bill asked for Captain David Spencer, but was told he was on a trip to Camp Savage, Minnesota—the new location of the army language school after its move from the Presidio. Bill handed his orders to the sergeant at the reception desk.

Three days of orientation followed. He endured a thorough physical examination, during which he managed to conceal the discomfort caused by the old ankle fracture. He filled out exactly eleven forms, which were submitted to seven different departments. From a list of recommended tailors, he chose one on Connecticut Avenue and ordered summer and winter uniforms. His tropical combat gear would be issued at his port of embarkation, San Diego.

The afternoon of the third day, Bill reported to Major Hutton, a staff psychologist, for what was called a "psychological evaluation." It was a tedious, exasperating interview; it lasted three hours and twenty minutes.

This was no interrogation about security matters. The army had already screened him for security and given Bill a top-secret clearance. Mostly, the interview focused on his feelings toward the

Japanese, which Captain David Spencer had also questioned.

Major Hutton was a hard-nosed psychologist who wasted few words. "You were born in a foreign country—with whom we are now at war. We have to be careful in deciding where to use you in our war effort."

"Why?"

"I'll ask the questions, Macneil. You just sit there and answer them."

"Screw that."

"Whaa—at?"

"Pardon my language, Major, but fuck that. I haven't taken my oath yet so I'm still a civilian. If I have questions to ask, I'll damned well ask them."

Major Hutton made busy notations on his pad, perhaps to cover his confusion.

"I asked you," Bill pressed on, "why you have to be especially careful about Americans born in foreign countries."

The major's face was flushed. "I think the answer is obvious. Americans born abroad may be less patriotic than those born at home."

"That's just what I thought, and it's ridiculous. The Caucasian Americans I knew who were born and raised in Japan were more loyal—if anything—to the United States than others."

"You said, 'Caucasian Americans.' Why make that distinction?"

"The Nisei are special. Having Japanese features, they are more readily accepted in Japanese society and may be more tempted to dilute their loyalties. People like me—Caucasians born and raised in Japan—are reminded every day of our lives there we are not Japanese, we are foreigners. The Japanese insist we can't understand them and that attitude itself is the highest barrier against our ever becoming a part of their world. They force us to keep on being foreign—in my case, American—whether we like it or not."

Bill knew he was going deeper into this subject than he should, but it was a sore point. "An American born and raised in, say, Siloam Springs, Arkansas, is not as conscious of his American nationality as I am. Nor does he face the frequent reminders of the differences between his country and others. I have seen a hundred ways in which Japan and America are different. I like America more, so I'll fight for her." Bill stopped for a moment. "I'm sorry if I sound like a political hack at a Fourth of July picnic, but that's how I feel."

After saying all that, Bill could not repress the memory of how close he had been to the Japanese families in their neighborhood—at least, before that winter he spent in Nanking. He could not deny they had accepted him as one of them while he was growing up.

The stocky, red-faced major hiccuped, then was busy for almost a minute making more notations. "That was quite a speech, Macneil, and it takes me on to the next section of the form, your feelings toward the Japanese. If I accept what you have just said as true, you love our country. Right? Now, just how much do you dislike the Japanese? This is important, because looking at your background and family situation, one might say you are practically Japanese yourself. I have been told, for example, that when you speak Japanese, you could pass for a native if your face were invisible."

"Don't worry about whether I hate them enough. I'll kill my share when I get out there."

"Listen to me, Macneil. We're at war with a tough enemy. A lot of our young men don't really know much about the Japanese. Unless our domestic propaganda can build up a lot of hatred in our guys, they may not be able to plunge a bayonet into a Jap stomach without hesitation or compunction. We want them to plunge that pigsticker in with a grin on their faces. To build up that much anger in an Iowa farm boy who has never done much more than wring a chicken's neck is what our propaganda machinery is working on right now. You've seen the posters. Slavering, cruel-looking Jap soldiers with buck teeth and slit-eyes behind Harold Lloyd glasses. Now *you* know the average Japanese doesn't look anything like that, but we've got to get that Iowa farm boy to think they do. That's why we're concerned about people like you. You're not going to accept those poster caricatures of the Japanese as real."

"Let me interrupt you, Major. I've told you I don't like the Japanese. At least, not their men—especially those in uniform. I assure you I will use that bayonet without any qualms."

"All right, so you've lived among them and speak their language and yet you say you hate them. Why?"

"For something they did in Nanking in 1937. I was only a boy, but I saw what they did in that Chinese town. I'll never forget it."

The major shifted to a more comfortable position in his swivel chair.

"What I want you to do, Macneil, is relax and tell me about Nanking. Take your time. I'll get you something to drink if you talk yourself dry. Go ahead."

Macneil leaned forward and began to speak slowly. This was not something he wanted to do, but the more he talked, the faster the words flowed. This was the first time he had told the whole story to anyone since 1937, but the scenes were still clearly etched in his memory. He found himself caught up in recounting those tragic events.

"I was fifteen and going to the American School in Tokyo. My best friend was another American named Mark Wood. He was in my class. His sister, Ellen, was there, too. She was a year younger than Mark. Ellen and I—we liked each other. Liked each other a lot, I guess. I was only fifteen, as I said, but I suppose we were sweethearts, although we were pretty young for that sort of thing.

"Mark's father taught English literature. He had been teaching at Aoyama Academy in Tokyo, but the year before he accepted an offer to teach the same subject at Nanking University in China. He wanted Mark and Ellen to finish high school in Tokyo, so he arranged for a place where they could get room and board and left them there. He asked my father to keep them out of trouble.

"Anyway, Mark and Ellen were going to Nanking early in December to spend Christmas that year and asked me and my sister Sarah to go with them. Sarah had other plans, but I went. I wasn't about to miss a chance to spend three weeks under the same roof with Ellen. Because of the war, my father wasn't sure about my going, but we didn't think the Japanese would bother us and we could get to Nanking by riverboat up the Yangtze from Shanghai. So we went."

Bill Macneil's narrative slowed as he looked out the major's window at the shimmering July heat waves.

"Take your time," Major Hutton said. "Want some water— or a cold drink?"

"No, I'm all right." Bill seemed to return to the present. "I was just thinking back. The Woods lived in what was called the "Safe Zone" in Nanking. Safe—what a laugh. But a lot of Chinese thought it was safe, too, and about two hundred thousand of them crowded into the zone in three days when the Japanese attacked.

"Chinese soldiers who surrendered to the Japanese were being massacred, so others threw away their uniforms and tried to pass as civilians. Well, the Japanese weren't having any of that, so they started driving all the Chinese men out of the safe zone over to the banks of the Yangtze, which we could see from the second floor of the Woods' home. The Chinese were lined up on the banks, and the Japanese machine guns opened up on them. When the barrels got too hot, the Japanese carried buckets of water from the river to cool them. It went on and on.

"That night the Japanese came back into the zone to get women. They raped some of them in the garden of the Woods' house. The next morning we saw the body of one of their Chinese maids in the garden. Her baby was dead beside her. It looked like a Japanese soldier had smothered the baby to keep it quiet, then raped and killed its mother.

"Ellen began to act funny after that. I guess we should have known something was wrong, but there was too much going on all around us.

"The raping and killing went on for days and days—from before Christmas to the end of January. We couldn't leave. The city was being looted and burned. Later we read estimates that about one hundred and fifty thousand men were executed, and five thousand women—some little girls—were raped. Much of this went on along the riverbanks, within our sight, and I guess it was just too much for Ellen. She must have decided—on her own—that she had to get out of Nanking. My God, she was only fourteen, but she was beginning—you know, to look like a woman. Maturing. Well, she left the house one night after we had all gone to bed and we didn't know she was gone till the next morning. Of course, Mr. and Mrs. Wood were frantic. There weren't any foreign soldiers we could rely on. When Mr. Wood tried to leave to go look for her, the Japanese drove him back inside with bayonets. But Mark and I—I guess because we were boys—got out and could move around. The Japanese were even friendly to us, especially when they found we spoke Japanese. Anyway, we went out searching for Ellen every day for nearly two weeks, but we never found her."

Bill stopped talking and let his chin sink to his chest.

"And she never was found?"

"She was found later, after I had gone back to Japan. She was with a missionary couple thirty miles west of Nanking. They said they found her wandering along a road. She was bruised and battered and nearly naked."

Bill's voice caught in his throat. "Ellen couldn't—or wouldn't—speak. In fact, she never spoke again, as far as I know. No one could find out what happened to her. She must have been raped, but she wouldn't let a doctor examine her, and her parents did not insist. They put her in a hospital in Shanghai and then she and her folks came home."

"Where is she now?"

"In a mental institution somewhere in New Hampshire."

After Bill Macneil took his oath as a newly minted captain in the military intelligence service, he traveled to Camp Savage, Minnesota, where he found David Spencer.

Several hundred Nisei were being trained in interrogation

and translation techniques at this isolated camp in the wilds of Minnesota. The men who might become members of Macneil's eight-man ATIS team in the South Pacific were among those in training. Spencer introduced him to Master Sergeant Kunio "Slats" Honda.

"Honda looks like a good man, Bill," Spencer told him later. "He's tough and he has a good grip on the language and he hates the Japanese as much as you do. I'm going to try to get him appointed to your team."

From Camp Savage, Macneil reported to Fort Benning, Georgia, for four weeks of training at the paratrooper school. He made ten practice jumps. In none of them did his weak ankle betray him.

In his new jump boots, with a blue paratrooper's badge on his uniform, Macneil made another of those interminable train journeys across the country to southern California to await embarkation to the Pacific.

chapter 11

Shanghai, China
August 1943

In early August Japanese defenses around Munda in the South Pacific had begun to collapse. By 20 August, Americans of the XIV Corps had routed remaining Japanese pockets on New Georgia.

Sarah Macneil knew Colonel Ishihara would not come to her Shanghai apartment that evening. The good colonel was playing mah-jongg until late with his cronies at the Japanese officers' club. That left Sarah free to bathe early and visit the Pootung Refugee Center.

It had been a muggy summer day in Shanghai. The office fans were not much help. In her apartment, conditions were more tolerable, with a breeze off the river wafting through open windows.

Mrs. Chang stood by while her mistress shed her damp clothing, bathed, and changed to a blue summer frock. The amah could not help admiring the gracefulness and agility of the well-proportioned young woman she had raised from babyhood.

Sarah reminded herself to offer a prayer of thanks for her loyal amah-san. Mrs. Chang was tall for a Chinese. She tied her hair in a tight bun and wore a white starched jacket with a high collar and black shiny pants. She said little but what she did say was strikingly to the point. She had glittering black eyes in a pockmarked face and her feet were large, because somehow she had been spared the torture of having her feet bound as a child.

"Will you eat something now or later?" Mrs. Chang asked.

"Later. I can take care of dinner myself. You go on downstairs." There was a dormitory arrangement for the servants in the basement of the apartment building.

"Is he coming?" Mrs. Chang referred to Colonel Ishihara, whom she despised.

"Not tonight." Sarah wished she could tell her amah that her true feelings for the colonel were not as they appeared to be. Mrs. Chang, however, was in her fifties and given to candid speech. Sarah could not risk revealing Nathan Blum was still the only man in her heart.

It was dark when Sarah unlocked Mrs. Chang's bicycle and started to pedal along the river toward the Pootung Refugee Center. Colonel Ishihara took strong exception to her bicycling along the streets and alleyways of Shanghai, but she was fast both on foot and on wheels and knew she could pass as a Chinese—as Lin Hsiao-mai, the identity stated on the door and mail box of her apartment.

The Pootung Center covered a huge area of crumbling buildings built by the Chiang Kai-shek government in the mid-thirties as a low-cost housing project. In its forty square blocks lived more than twelve thousand Manchurian Jews. The rest of the refugees from Manchuria had been settled in other segregated areas like Honkew and Lunghwa.

Entire families lived in single rooms. Many windowpanes were broken and some warped doors would not close. Toilets were outside; kitchens were communal. Drinking water had to be purchased from passing vendors. The inhabitants froze in winter and stifled in summer.

Yet, Sarah loved visiting Pootung. There was a hard-to-describe Jewish atmosphere—formed by music, voices, pleasant aromas—that reminded her of Nathan. She felt she was communing with his spirit there. And, of course, it was there she found opportunities to fulfill her pledge to her dying fiancé.

The Japanese guards knew her on sight and usually passed her through without a glance at the pass signed by Colonel Ishihara. Many of the Jews, if they noticed her at all, assumed she was a Chinese functionary carrying out minor errands for the Japanese officer who was chief refugee camp administrator. Ishihara knew about her visits to Pootung, for she reported faithfully to him on the conditions she observed there.

Sarah had found it easy to persuade Ishihara to order improvements in the lot of the Jews. He was, after all, a humane man who was a far cry from the virulently anti-Semitic Gerhardt Kahner, Gestapo chief in the Shanghai region. But Ishihara was confronted by restrictions and shortages. With Japan's war-time economy not always able to produce enough for her own soldiery, the supplies allocated to refugee areas and POW encampments throughout Asia were sometimes less than minimal.

Sarah had found the best way to help the Pootung inhabitants was to report an intolerable situation to the colonel that, if left unattended, would quickly worsen and become a cause for embarrassment. Potable water was a case in point. When in short supply, illness spread. Deaths mounted. Burial details streamed out of the Pootung gates. The International Red Cross and missionaries from neutral nations began to nose about.

Sarah was learning how to achieve her humanitarian objectives without leaving her lover with the impression she was an all-out advocate of the welfare of the Jewish refugees. She would say, "Well, if we do this, here is the outcome. If we don't, then we may have a serious problem." That did not always work, but it was effective often enough to justify her continuing it.

With Ishihara's approval, she had approached the Sassoon family of Shanghai for five additional tons of rice during one period when the usual supply channels were clogged. The Sassoons were Iraqi Jews not subject to Japanese restrictions. At least, not yet. Once, she had heard of a shipment of badly needed medicines being brought to Shanghai by a Swedish medical missionary group. To prevent the valuable supplies from being pilfered on the unloading docks, Ishihara had—at Sarah's urgent behest—assigned a squad of Japanese marines with fixed bayonets to watch the coolies. A Swedish female missionary stood by with tears of gratitude streaming down her cheeks.

And, of course, Pootung received a large share of that medicine.

In late spring of that year, Sarah set out to locate some of the Chinese who had worked in the Shanghai office of the Macneil hong. She found five. The hong office had closed right after hostilities began, but the five ex-employees were willing to cooperate with Sarah.

With the help of these five Chinese men, Sarah planned—if exigencies demanded—to mount an operation both daring and heroic. Its essence was to arm the Pootung Jews—or arm enough of them—to fight their way out of the refugee camp toward the west.

Sarah spent many evenings when not with Ishihara thinking about the perils besetting the people she had come to think of as "her Jews."

Their danger from the Japanese was unpredictable. While Ishihara leaned toward humane treatment of the Jews, his superior General Doihara was indifferent. Mostly, the Japanese forces in China, as well as the government at home, thought of these refugees, if they thought of them at all, as an annoyance. They had no reason to inflict harm on the Jews, but neither would they expend much on saving them from harm.

The Germans were a different story. Gerhardt Kahner advocated the "Final Solution" and was supported by the German ambassador, Heinrich Stahmer. Fortunately for the Jews, Ishihara detested the Gestapo chief. So far, German influence in China was nominal.

As Sarah saw it, the danger lay in what might be negotiated between Berlin and Tokyo. The Germans were fighting their war in Europe, in Africa, and on the high seas, while the Japanese theaters of combat were Asia and the Pacific. The Japanese armies along the Siberian border tied up many Soviet divisions, but even if the Wehrmacht had not been mired in Russia, the Japanese would still have kept their rifles and cannon aimed at the Russians across from northern Manchuria.

Diplomatic cables flew back and forth between the Foreign Ministry in Tokyo and Japan's embassy in Berlin. Even Ishihara, who had been closely involved in the Richard Sorge spy case, had heard disturbing rumors; one recent report said the Japanese navy and air force were desperately in need of some Uranium-235. Unable to find any in China or Korea, they were pleading with Germany to provide them with a shipment by submarine.

Just how desperate Japan's need was for uranium—and why, Ishihara had wondered aloud one evening in Sarah's bed. Pretending indifference, she had turned over to go to sleep, but then an alarm bell rang in her mind. What if the Nazis offered Japan a deal? "We will give you the uranium you require if you will turn over to us the German-Jews in China."

It was obvious to Sarah the Germans could not transport several thousand Jews back to Germany. If they were to apply the "Final Solution," it would have to be done right in Shanghai. Since they were "processing" thousands of Jews every day in the death camps in Poland, it would not take more than a couple of weeks to eliminate Sarah's Jews, provided a crematorium was built.

Ishihara's office would know in advance of any such danger. What Sarah hoped to do was arm the Jews and lead them out of Shanghai westward to a junction somewhere with the Chinese Communist forces who would, of course, be resolutely opposed to anything the Germans proposed. It would be risky and she still had discovered no way to obtain weapons, but she saw that as the only way she could rescue a sizable percentage of the Pootung people from the deadly intentions of the Nazis.

Before leaving Pootung later that evening, Sarah paid a visit to one family of German Jews to whom she had become very attached. Maybe it was because the aesthetic father reminded her so much of Nathan. Also, she doted on the two darling children to whom she sometimes brought candy or toys.

This Dresden family welcomed her visits and accepted her as

what she said she was—a Chinese aide to Colonel Ishihara. Although they may have wondered, they did not openly question why she had singled them out for her affectionate attentions. The children clung to Sarah and always begged her to stay longer. She did, in fact, spend several nights with them on a mat in the corner, when Ishihara was away from Shanghai with General Doihara.

Sarah was summoned to the colonel's office early the following afternoon. He was at his desk, in shirt sleeves, wiping his face and neck with an o-shibori towel. He did not smile, and Sarah sensed this was to be strictly a business meeting.

"Where were you last night? I called your apartment, but there was no answer."

"I went to Pootung, sir, on an inspection. I'm writing a report on the visit."

"And Mrs. Chang?"

"I assume she was downstairs in the maids' dormitory."

"I was worried."

"I didn't see the general, if that's what you mean." Sarah knew Ishihara was wildly jealous—and that he found himself in a most delicate position. Doihara could easily have the colonel transferred to a jungle fighting unit in the South Pacific.

Ishihara seemed to get a grip on himself, returning to his usual devil-may-care attitude. He filled his pipe and lit it. This was a new affectation begun after he received a fine set of pipes from Victor Kahdrie, another Iraqi Jew. He passed a list of names to Sarah.

"Do you know any of these?" he asked.

The list contained six names, apparently Jewish. Sarah Macneil knew none of them and said so.

"No? Well, you will get to know them."

"Will you be good enough to explain?"

"These German Jews are all scientists. Some were professors; others researchers. All are well-known in the field of nuclear physics. We have orders to send them to Tokyo—to the Rikken Laboratory."

"Are they all in Pootung?"

Ishihara nodded, leaning back in his chair.

"And what am I to do with this list?"

"You, my dear, are to escort all six of them to Tokyo."

"Must I? I would really rather stay here . . . with you." She formed her lips into a pout she knew reminded him of a certain sex act. She arched her eyebrows in triangles of surprise under her newly cropped hair. Her eyes were glowing with a frank invitation. She knew how seductive she was to him. She also knew he was secretly pleased to send her away from Shanghai—and the possible attentions of General Doihara—for a while. He would rather be deprived of her sexual acrobatics than tormented by jealous suspicions of whatever crafty ruses Doihara might be employing to meet Sarah behind his back.

"Go find these people and get them ready for the trip. Tell them you don't know how long they will be gone. Their families—if they have families—will be taken care of. You'll leave in three days. A plane will take you. Top-priority travel orders are being cut. You will travel, of course, as Lin Hsiao-mai, so be sure you have your certificate of Chinese citizenship with you, just in case."

Ishihara paused thoughtfully. "At times I wish we did not have to pretend you are Chinese. By the way, where is your American passport?"

"In my home in Tokyo."

"Hmmm. It would be better if we could tear it up and get you a Japanese passport. You might talk to your grandfather at the Foreign Ministry about that while you are in Tokyo. But if he gets one for you, leave it in Tokyo. You're already accepted down here as a Chinese, so let's not muddy the waters."

Two days after Sarah and her six German-Jewish scientists left Shanghai, Colonel Ishihara flew into a rage. He had been tricked. General Doihara had gone by train to Peking and from Peking he too had flown to Tokyo.

Ishihara's first thought was to hurry to Tokyo himself, but he knew he could not leave his post without the general's authorization.

chapter 12

Tokyo, Japan
October 1943

The Japanese bases at Lae and Salamaua, New Guinea, had fallen in September, although the people of Japan did not know that.

October was a good month in Japan. The dog days of summer were past, as well as the uncertainties of the typhoon season. A Japanese proverb spoke happily of horses fattening under blue autumnal skies, although Helma was not sure why the Japanese would prize obesity in their horses. Surely they did not eat them. Or did they?

One of Helma's two jobs at Radio Tokyo gave her access to knowledge about the war's progress. The Kyodo Monitoring Service received shortwave broadcasts from the United States and provided Radio Tokyo with transcripts of the newscasts. Helma Graf did not agree with much Captain Horace Milmay did, or attempted to do, in their broadcasting to the American and Allied forces fighting in the miserable jungles of the South Pacific, but in this case she made an exception. One of her two regular broadcasts was, she thought, a superb inspiration: one with which she had no quarrel.

Milmay's idea was that Japan should see to it that uniformed Americans were provided with word of disasters, strikes, epidemics, and widespread loss of life of any origin in America. All of this was aired without embellishment or editorializing—virtually verbatim as received from the United States. The soldiers and sailors would want to know of such events and would learn later, in letters from home, that the news programs from Japan were to be trusted (although, of course, the Japanese propaganda transmissions were not).

Accurately enough, Milmay calculated that bad news from home would sadden and worry the fighting men and perhaps diminish the intensity of their fighting spirit. In fact, that calculation was shared by the Allied high command, which permitted only occasional sanitized versions of bad news from home to reach the ears of the men in combat. Surely, the fighting men had more than enough on their minds.

Helma approved of these broadcasts because they were entirely truthful and because she was willing to do her part to discourage the Americans from further slaughter, much as she wanted to discourage the Japanese from all hostilities.

But it was her other regular program, also aired weekly, that she fought continually with Horace Milmay about.

Two days earlier, Helma had politely placed on Milmay's desk a proposed transcript of her second program.

"I'm sorry, sir, but I won't announce this program as written."

The Englishman's face became mottled with fury. "I wrote that myself. What exactly do you find objectionable?" His sarcasm was palpable.

Helma picked up the three typewritten pages. "Well, I remember making the broadcast about American GIs sending home Japanese skulls as souvenirs, and we know it was true, because we got it by shortwave from Los Angeles. But I think you go too far in your comments. The Americans are not that depraved."

Milmay was barely able to keep his temper in check. "Which comments are those?"

"Here you want me to say, 'These barbaric acts can be traced to the brutal nature rooted deep in the national character of the American people as well as their superiority complex toward Asiatics. Similar cases are not difficult to find in American history. The massacre of the Indians, the lynching of Negroes, the—' "

"I recognize the comments. Let me remind you, Helma—"

"Miss Graf, if you don't mind." There was a new tartness in her voice.

"Very well, *Miss Graf*, if that is how you prefer it. I would remind you that you were not employed to pass judgment on the suitability of the words you are expected to read."

"That is quite true, Captain Milmay, but let me remind you I am a Swiss national. A citizen of a neutral nation. If I am not permitted a certain discretion in the messages I am supposed to speak, I will take up the matter with Baron Matsui. If he supports your view, I will quit Radio Tokyo."

Very close to sputtering, Milmay's face was flushed with blood. Helma was delighted that he was as angry as she had ever seen him. With a flip of her blond hair, she spun on her heels and started toward the door of his office.

"You come back here. I did not give you permission to leave."

"I'm leaving anyway—unless you allow me to make changes in this transcript. Extensive changes."

After a moment the Englishman heaved a stertorous sigh. "All right, all right. Ink in your damnable changes and bring them back to me. But hurry! This must go on the air this evening and I still have to get the baron to initial it."

"That won't be possible, Captain. The baron has gone riding at the Imperial Palace stables. He won't be back in his office until tomorrow."

Milmay eyed her suspiciously. "How do you know that?"

"He told me so last night." With that Helma departed.

Walking along the corridor and down the stairs, Helma Graf grinned to herself. She really shouldn't tell fibs like that. True, the baron had given her a ride home in his famous gold Packard, but it was right after work. The baron's mansion was a short distance beyond the Macneil home in Azabu, and he was often kind enough to give her a lift, at least when he had enough gasoline to run his fancy car. Most Japanese automobiles had already been converted to charcoal as fuel, which Matsui would not countenance.

If Milmay wanted to think she had a date with the widowed baron, Helma didn't mind at all. She even wished now she had accepted one of the baron's invitations to go dancing at the Florida, which had closed recently due to the wartime exigencies.

In autumn 1943, Radio Tokyo was filled with people Helma found to be strange, yet fascinating. Perhaps the strangest was Baron Nobutaka Matsui, a man she might be very fond of—if not for Bill Macneil, who might even now be fighting for his life in the Pacific.

The baron was known in Japan as the "playboy of the Eastern

world." He was forty-two and came from a samurai background, although he disapproved of what he termed the "ridiculous ideals of the Code of Bushido." His grandfather, the baron cheerfully admitted, had been what was called a "*shoben samurai*": a "piss samurai" or warrior of the lowest grade. Through a great stroke of luck and not a little chicanery, his grandfather had built the foundation of a modest fortune through the acquisition—probably illegal—of a copper mine near the town of Ashikaga, north of Tokyo. His son, the present baron's father, had acquired other nearby mining properties and promoted a modest fortune into a magnificent one, with the baronetcy coming along in due course.

When Nobutaka Matsui became an officer in the army, he soon discovered he was far more interested in fast cars and motorboats and fine horseflesh than military duties.

With his horse, Uranus, he competed throughout Europe in the early thirties and in the 1936 Olympics won a gold medal for Japan in the individual jump event. In Hollywood he was perceived as a dashing fellow: daring on the polo field, irresistible in the bedroom, and unquenchable at the bar.

In 1938 he returned to his baroness in Japan with the gold-painted, 12-cylinder Packard in the hold of the ship.

When his wife died in 1940, Matsui began to give more serious attention to his long-ignored military obligations, only to find his fellow cavalry officers resented his playboy image and his publicly expressed contempt for samurai ideals. Unable to dislodge him from his position of affection in the eyes of the emperor, the army got him out of its hair by arranging to have Matsui assigned a desk job as chief of the Foreign Broadcast Division of Radio Tokyo. There the baron became, in effect, Japan's chief propagandist although he had not the slightest doubt, as he had confided to Helma during one of their rides home from work, that Japan would be beaten to a pulp—as he put it—in this stupid war.

Although a brave and patriotic Japanese, the baron was no war lover. He was, in fact, writing a song to be called the "*Gumba Koshin-kyoku*" or the "Military Horse March." The lyrics contained a number of rather subtle anti-war messages, which warmed Helma's heart toward him.

What if he asked her to go dancing somewhere besides the now-defunct Florida? Helma feared she would give in to that temptation, so she tried to steer their conversations away from music and dancing.

Traditional Quakers frowned on music. Helma Graf did her best to suppress her love of song, as well as that sometimes irresistible desire to lose herself in the mesmerizing strains of the tango. Music and dance felt too much like that other tingling desire—the one she felt coursing through her body but would not allow herself to confront sincerely.

Besides Baron Nobutaka Matsui and the despised Captain Horace Milmay, other *rara avis* of assorted plumage were toiling in the drab Radio Tokyo building. These included thirteen Allied POWs who had worked in radio stations elsewhere in civilian life, but only one was an out-and-out traitor like Milmay. Most performed technical jobs, and although they would surely be interrogated by their own military authorities at the conflict's end, it was perhaps unlikely that they would be charged with the serious crime of collaboration with the enemy. That, at least, was their frequently voiced opinion among themselves.

The group to which Helma Graf belonged was the announcers: nineteen women and four men. Two men were Japanese born but raised in America. The third was a Filipino who had worked in radio in Manila and was captured by the Japanese after he joined the Philippine Scouts. The fourth was a Caucasian American from Kansas, the only ally Milmay had on the entire staff.

The nineteen female announcers were a mixed bag. Helma Graf was the only national from a neutral country. One, Iva Toguri, was an American Nisei who refused to renounce her American citizenship and who remained dangerously supportive of the American side throughout her term of employment. Like Helma Graf, Iva often tried to modulate any anti-American venom expressed in her particular program scripts and had been castigated for her attempts.

Milmay would have liked to get rid of the Swiss woman for her intransigence and would have done so had he not suspected Baron Matsui had become intimate with Helma. On the other hand, Milmay tried to protect Iva Toguri. Milmay had chosen her to be the premier attraction of the "Zero Hour" because her voice was such a contrast to the soft, mellifluous tones of the other women. He was confident the targeted audience would perk up its ears, remember Iva's voice, and perhaps even get to like it.

The English captain proved to be correct. Iva did gain in popularity among her listeners. Upon their arrival at prison camps in Japan, recently captured GIs pleaded for radios so they could continue to listen to the woman they had come to call "Tokyo Rose," a name never used by anyone at Radio Tokyo and unknown to the staff until just recently.

Without doubt, Iva Toguri was the star performer, and she was kept on the payroll despite her disquieting pro-American sentiments. Her popularity grew among Allied servicemen and with it, so did Milmay's stature at Radio Tokyo. He wanted to keep her on and was able to do so even though Iva was, in fact, an enemy alien: an American who was relatively candid about her preferences.

On the other hand, Helma Graf was neither anti-American nor pro-Japanese. She was for everyone and against no one. And she held a trump card none of the others had. She could walk away from her job at any time.

The other women on the announcing staff included Ruth Sumi Hayakawa, born in Japan but resident in America after the age of two; June Yoshie Suyama, born in Japan but raised in Canada; and Margaret Yaeko Kato, Japan-born but reared in England. All three were Japanese citizens without qualification.

Three Nisei had dual citizenship: Katherine Kei Fujiwara, Mieko Furuya, and Kaoru Morooka. As citizens of both Japan and the United States but living in the former, they found it was Japan in effective control of their destinies and their apparent loyalties.

On the air, none of these women ever identified themselves with their true names and none ever used the term "Tokyo Rose." Helma, however, wanted a broadcast name and finally got one from Baron Matsui.

She had begun to read aloud a script for the approval of the indifferent baron one day. At the top of the first page was the word "Ann"—a typist's abbreviation of "Announcer." Helma read the word as "Ann" instead of "Announcer," which caught Matsui's flagging attention.

"You've been wanting a name, haven't you, Helma? Why don't you call yourself Ann?"

"That's just an abbreviation for—"

"I know, I know, but why not?"

Helma embellished Matsui's idea with the word "orphan." The other announcers had sometimes called their GI listeners the "orphans of the Pacific" to emphasize that the Washington brass were more supportive of the war in Europe than the one in the distant jungles and lonely beaches of the Pacific. "Hi, you orphans of the Pacific! This is another little orphan in Tokyo: Little Orphan Ann. Now how about a number by Bonnie Baker?"

After a few broadcasts Helma changed "Ann" to "Annie," because of her fondness for the comic strip she grew up reading—and from which she had adopted slang such as "jeepers."

Helma's Friday night program was expanded to one hour and always began with a recording of the Boston Pops playing "Strike Up the Band." Next "Ann" relayed messages from POWs garnered from prisoner-of-war camps in Japan: "Hi, Mom. This is your boy Private Tom Edison. I'm all right, but I sure do need some warm socks. Tell the Winthrops their son Allen is in the same camp with me. He's okay, too."

Next, Orphan Annie would switch to her disc jockey role with recordings of popular or semi-classical music. She prefaced these with pert comments of her own and always seemed to be joking: "Did you like that, fellows? Anyway, here I am, alert and smiling. Has my radiant personality electrified all of you guys? What's that? No? Aw, shucks, you fellow orphans. Give a gal a break, won't you? I'm not really your bitter enemy, you know. Just a lonesome gal dreaming of her sweetheart. Just like you're dreaming of some sweet little thing back home in the good ole U.S. of A., am I right? What? You didn't know I had a sweetheart? I do, you know. And I think you would be very, very surprised to know where he is. Maybe a whole lot closer to you than you think. You wanta know his name? I think it would embarrass him if I told you, so I'll just call him Bill, okay?"

What different worlds, Helma thought as she was returning home one night when she was not scheduled for an evening broadcast. If Bill Macneil really was in the Pacific, how hot it must be there. Here in Tokyo, even in the mild month of October, it was sometimes cold at night, all residential gas having been cut off earlier in the year. The Macneil household was heating with charcoal braziers like everyone else. Heating a bath with firewood was tiresome so Helma usually went to the public bath, which was, at best, lukewarm and where she was stared at even on the women's side of the bathhouse. Then she reminded herself Bill might be bathing out of his helmet in cold salt water.

In the Azabu mansion Helma made sure Umeko was being taken care of, then changed into slacks, sweater, and a light coat. She picked up her *zatsuno*—the haversack everyone was required to carry these days to leave hands free for emergencies—and walked down the hill to the shops in Juban-gai. She stood in line for fifty minutes waiting to buy carrots only to have the green-grocer shout he had sold out when she was third in line.

Frustrated, she began the long walk to the Swiss Embassy. The offices would not be open, but some of her friends might be willing to share their larders. Every day it seemed some other product disappeared from the shelves or began to be rationed. Firewood and charcoal. Soap, matches, shoes, and thread. Milk, sugar, and fresh fish. (The smelly dried fish was plentiful, unfortunately.) Oil, meat, eggs.

Helma received a 10-ounce bread ration a day with a little salt and soy bean gruel. And that was more than Japanese civilians got. What kept her household alive was Umeko's special invalid rations, which required a physician's certificate, and what scanty canned goods she managed to cadge from the Swiss Embassy.

Their plight was clearly illustrated because Helma could count the ribs of the mice that tottered across the garden. Even the family cat, Mi-chan, lacked the energy to chase them.

Later that night Helma crept into Bill's bed, lit the *andon*—the night lamp—and penned a brief letter to the previous occupant of that sleeping space: "Dearest, Thy sister was here. She brought to Tokyo six nuclear physicists who had been in a camp in Shanghai. I will send thee her Shanghai address with my next letter. Right now I am too weary to try to find it. I love thee. Helma."

She had one comforting thought before falling asleep. Neither she nor Umeko nor Shipton had used much of the cash entrusted to each of them by Neil Macneil before he left Japan. They all had agreed to keep the money for emergencies and for the harder times they knew would come.

The Four Horsemen had begun to lead their steeds out of the stable.

CHAPTER 13

Tokyo, Japan
December 1943

Two years already? Had the war really been going on that long?

Dr. Chinda Nishikawa found that hard to believe. Except at Midway, Japan had piled up victory after victory at first, but that tide was turning. Of course, the public did not know, and even most of the fools in power were practicing mass deception—on themselves.

But Nishikawa knew. He knew, very well.

They could talk all they wanted about moral superiority and the power of the spirit, but Napoleon Bonaparte had been right. God was on the side of the heaviest battalions.

He sat on the tatami, his legs enveloped in a warm kotatsu, sipping his banshaku—his evening libation of rice-wine. He held out his cup for the ex-geisha at his side to fill.

She, at least, was a satisfactory change. His previous mistress had simply not been to his taste. She was not as abandoned between the futon as he liked. He kept urging her to put more spirit into her work, but she merely whimpered instead of yelling. And she absolutely refused to do some of the more unorthodox acts he demanded.

For example, that delightful trick with the egg.

No matter. Now that the government had banned places of entertainment, the geishas in Tokyo—all 3,500—were out of work, hungrily seeking other employment. The jobs they were most qualified for were sinecures as courtesans, so it was a buyer's market. This woman was the second Nishikawa had agreed to take on for a trial period, and he thought she might work out. At least, she was vocal enough to suit him in her between-the-futon endeavors.

"Is my bath ready?"

The kimono-clad woman bowed, her forehead almost touching the tatami. "I'm sorry. The water is not as hot as you like it, master. We ran out of firewood today."

Chinda Nishikawa exploded—and slapped her. "Why didn't you buy more?" he snarled.

She bowed again. "There's no—no money, master."

"You fool! Why didn't you say so? Here, take this and go get wood. Now!"

The ex-geisha slunk fearfully to the sliding door, knelt, and bowed again, then hurried out.

At this rate, she won't be with me long, Nishikawa thought. But no problem; he could find a replacement in short order. That would be the least of his concerns.

What did concern him was Japan's fate. With his aid, the Rikken Laboratory just might be Japan's best chance—perhaps only chance—for victory. If only he could succeed in constructing several nuclear bombs. . . .

He had been on the verge of tossing in the spoon, as the Japanese would say, until recently, but the six Jewish nuclear physicists from Shanghai had changed his mind. Now he knew how it could be done. He was ninety-five percent certain of success.

Refilling his sake cup, he remembered the young woman who had brought the Shanghai Jews to Rikken; who had argued long and hard with the laboratory director until it was agreed they would be guaranteed decent living conditions.

He wished she had stayed in Tokyo. He would rather have installed her in an apartment than any of the ex-geisha he had interviewed. There was something about her that tantalized Nishikawa unbearably. That bold face. The black eyes glittering with intelligence. The body that seemed alive with extraordinary energy. Someone said she was the granddaughter of an ambassador. She used a Chinese name—Lin something—but spoke Japanese of native quality. Maybe she had both Chinese and Japanese blood. He liked mixed-bloods.

From Germany, Rikken had received a submarine shipment of 100 kilos of natural uranium. Nishikawa had enriched its U-235 content by 20 percent, thus producing fissionable uranium in which a chain reaction could be initiated.

Nishikawa knew that when an atom of U-235 fissioned, neutrons would start the chain reaction. The Rikken cyclotron could cause that fission by firing neutrons at the enriched uranium.

One of the Jewish physicists from Shanghai had taught Nishikawa how to introduce a "moderator" to reduce the amount of enriched uranium needed. One of the best moderators, the physicist said, was deuterium, or heavy water, for which Dr. Nishikawa had located a source in Konan, the Goliath-sized industrial complex sprawling 72 miles along the northeast coast of Korea.

With heavy water in hand, Nishikawa was confident he could achieve his goal—a controlled atomic reaction.

If only he could arm his country with a handful of uranium bombs—now being called atomic bombs by some—before it was too late. . . .

But enough of that for tonight. He could hear his new mistress removing the wooden lid from the bathtub. He would tell her to climb into the steamy hot water with him and wash his back and then—

Chapter 14

New Guinea (North Coast)
December 1943

After Greenland, New Guinea was the second largest island on earth. Bill Macneil was sure it was the hottest.

It was a strange land of amazing extremes. Massive 16,000-foot mountains towered over a 1,200-mile northern coastline dotted with tenacious Japanese strongholds. All the way, sheer cliffs alternated with nipa and mangrove swamps that sucked everyone's feet into mire. In the sorrowful words of Douglas MacArthur, New Guinea was "one of the most formidable obstacles to military operations" ever known to man.

Approaching by plane, New Guinea showed the newcomer its better side: a sparkling blue tropic sea aglow with phosphorescence at night, craggy off-shore islands, long, *long* beaches, plunging gorges, impenetrable jungles thick with parasites.

From thousands of feet up, it offered one of the most beautiful tropical scenes on the planet. And if the first-time visitor was fortunate enough to land at an upland town like Wau, he would find a settlement with incomparable climate, no mosquitoes, and comfortable cottages surrounded by lovely gardens.

Altitude often spelled the difference, because the temperature became increasingly bearable after one climbed 100 feet above sea level. While altitude meant a lot, it did not mean all. At considerable altitude on nearby Manus Island could be found a village that was filthy, squalid, and almost unlivable. Its name: Bali-ha'i.

Descending from 6000 feet to ground level was akin to descending from paradise into a gloomy, pestilential hellhole, where malignant vines seized the intruder and the ground teemed with insects.

When Bill Macneil's big Douglas C-54 Skymaster landed on the rutted, rocky airstrip and a crewman had opened the door, the ATIS captain had started down the ladder to find the heat instantly intolerable, like the explosion of fiery air that gushes from a blast furnace. In seconds, the heat seared the sweat from his body and left him so weak he staggered stepping off the bottom of the ladder. Panting, Bill took a firmer grip on his gear and stumbled toward a shack beside the runway, his eight-man team of interpreters and translators gasping along behind him.

That was in early September, after months of waiting in Australia. Four months after their landing, Macneil and his team were still on New Guinea although farther up the coast, inching toward the Philippines.

Elsewhere, in the Marshall Islands, Tarawa was being invaded.

Macneil had just walked into the tent of the commanding officer of the 158th RCT (Regimental Combat Team), Colonel Sam Neuhoff—a bear of a man with porcine features and a shaved head. Macneil was gaunt, burned by the sun, and dressed in combat fatigues with rolled-up sleeves.

"Sir, Captain William Macneil, Military Intelligence, reporting for duty. I brought an ATIS team with me."

"ATIS? What the fuck is that?"

"Allied Translator and Interpreter Service, sir. As you requested."

"Yeah, right. You came in yesterday with that bunch of Nips."

Here we go again, Macneil thought, taking a deep breath. "Colonel, my men are Americans and I'll ask you to not to call them Nips—or Japs."

"They look like Japs to me, and I'll call them whatever I fucking well please."

"You do that, Colonel, and I'll send a radio today getting me and my team assigned elsewhere. There are a hell of a lot of other units like yours, with a ton of enemy documents, begging for one of our teams. I won't have my men working where they are treated like the enemy." Macneil picked up the orders he had just placed in front of the colonel. He saluted with his middle finger sticking out conspicuously and spun on his heels.

That evening, in one of the two ATIS team's tents, Bill was writing out a request for team transfer, which he would have sent to ATIS Headquarters in Indooroopilly, Australia. Master Sergeant Kunio "Slats" Honda entered and sat in a chair next to Bill's desk. There was no longer much formality between the two.

"Captain, the shit really hit the fan today. They say you could hear Colonel Neuhoff squealing like a stuck hog."

"I didn't like his damn attitude. I just told him—"

Slats Honda grinned. "I know what you told him. It's all over camp. His top sergeant was listening outside the tent. He told me—and everyone else."

Honda was short, sturdy, and cocky. His parents, who had

immigrated to America from Wakayama Prefecture, ran a restaurant called "Frankie's" in Fresno, California. Wanting to get away from greasy kitchen smells, Honda had joined the U.S. Army in 1940 and had worked his way up to master sergeant by the time of Pearl Harbor. He was a *kibei*, having spent three years in a Wakayama middle school in the thirties. He could not remember where he picked up the nickname Slats.

"That reminds me, Captain," Honda said. "Here's something the boys wanted me to give you. It's something they liberated last week. I don't drink this gook stuff myself, but they tell me it's real good."

Macneil accepted the gift. It was a bottle of Hakutsuru *Tokkyu*—Special-Grade White Crane sake. "It's good, all right. Real good. Tell them we'll all drink it together—soon. What's the occasion?"

The Nisei sergeant seemed embarrassed. After a moment of hesitation, he said, "Well, the guys were a little—you know—standoffish from you at first. Almost hostile, you might say. You know, the Nisei resent you white officers because you got commissions and we didn't. We didn't like that, especially when most of us know more Japanese than you guys do."

"I can understand that, Slats."

"But then we found out you know better Japanese than us, and on top of that you started really going to bat for us—like today—so we just wanted to say—well, thanks."

Like Bill's, the other ATIS teams were having to fight for acceptance throughout the South Pacific. It wasn't bad enough many of their relatives were in relocation centers in the deserts of the American West, now they were finding that many ignorant servicemen saw their Japanese faces and assumed they were

"Japs." On two occasions it was only through Macneil's last-minute intervention that members of his team had been saved from serious injury or even death at the hands of other Allied soldiers. Like Colonel Neuhoff, they assumed a Jap was a Jap who should be exterminated on sight.

"You know how I feel about you and your men, Sergeant." Macneil picked up the radio message he had just finished. "By the way, will you carry this over to the communications tent and tell them to send it to our headquarters?"

"Is this about our transfer, sir?"

Macneil nodded, leaning back in his chair.

Honda handed the message back. "No need to send it, sir. Colonel Neuhoff sends word he wants you and your team of—" the Nisei smiled, "—*Americans* to start doing translation and interpreting right away."

Macneil enjoyed a moment of grim satisfaction. Major victories could come from an accumulation of minor ones. "All right, Sergeant. Unpack our gear. Get the dictionaries out on the tables. Let's have at it early tomorrow. Maybe we can clear away all this work in a week or two."

Since coming to New Guinea, Macneil and his team had been assigned successively to six military units: the 24th, 40th, and 41st army divisions, the 5th Marines, and two RCTs.

Each duty assignment had been pretty much the same. Move in and set up. Collect diaries, letters, maps, and other papers—sometimes too blood-drenched to read—for Macneil to glance at and assign priorities to. Sergeant Honda would divide up the work among the seven team members. When one of the enlisted men found a document he couldn't read, he would take it to Honda, and if the sergeant did not know the characters or the style of writing, he would bring it to Bill.

Depending on how many Japanese they had killed, some units might have thousands of documents, especially diaries, which the Japanese army did not forbid its men from keeping, probably believing none of these personal memoirs—many of them written in grass-writing, or *sosho*—would be intelligible to the barbarians. Because of the sheer volume, Macneil did not ask that any of the diaries or letters from home be completely translated. His men skimmed them looking for unit designations, strengths, and orders to move, or about conditions in the homeland. Military orders and maps were, of course, treated more thoroughly.

All intelligence of local tactical interest was given to the division or regiment that captured the document. Summaries or distillations were bundled up with the complete document and sent by courier back to ATIS headquarters.

His team's most outstanding achievement was translation of a map that gave soundings in a bay on the north coast of New Britain. These soundings were much deeper than those on the 1890s chart in the possession of MacArthur's staff. Recognizing that more and larger warships could use that sheltered bay as an anchorage, MacArthur was able to hasten his advance northwest to the Philippines by three weeks.

POW interrogation was an integral part of the ATIS team's duties, but so far it had not become onerous. Only a few Japanese had been captured, and many of them were so badly wounded, they were only semi-conscious when brought to Macneil.

Honda and Macneil questioned those who were not wounded. Usually they worked together, first softening up the prisoner with a cigarette or two and some casual conversation. Most of the

Japanese were country boys, despondent at being captured, sullen and uncooperative. Just persuading them to give their names and unit numbers could be a monumental task, and sometimes Macneil gave up and sent them back to the POW pen, to try again later. Often, however, getting the unit number out of a clamped-shut mouth would provide the opening wedge. Bill— and Slats, too—knew enough about Japanese army divisions to be aware of which prefecture most of their POWs came from. The Japanese 6th Division, for instance, was a hard-fighting unit from Kumamoto Prefecture in Kyushu. When one POW gave the 6th as his unit, Macneil, who had once spent a week in Kumamoto, began to reminisce happily about scenic Mount Aso and the marvelous hot spring resorts at its base. In a few minutes there was the suspicion of tears in the prisoner's eyes and after one more cigarette he opened up.

When Honda asked the prisoner about the 6th Division's order of battle, the man had no idea what he was talking about, but when Macneil asked about artillery dispositions, a light of understanding dawned, and he pointed out on a map where there were three batteries of "Kyunana-shiki Kyokusha Hokeiho" or 97-model high-angle infantry field pieces that fired eighty-one millimeter shells.

Hearing that, Macneil said he had to go to the *kawaya* for a moment—using Japanese slang meaning "head," which brought a smile to the prisoner's face—and hurried to the other team tent. He called Tech. Sergeant Ben Maeda aside and gave him a note to take on the double to RCT headquarters.

That afternoon, those enemy batteries were destroyed by mortar fire and after that, the colonel seemed to have even less trouble thinking of Macneil's men as Americans.

The same POW also revealed that two Nambu machine-gun emplacements were running very low on ammunition, which resulted in a probe and a successful night attack by one of the RCT platoons.

The ATIS team worked in two large pyramidal tents with their canvas sides rolled up for ventilation. Inside, the eight men sweated among the fourteen team dictionaries of military terms, Japanese names, kanji characters and compounds, nautical words, and medical terminology.

The work was drudgery—until one of the men jumped up with a letter or diary and rushed to find Captain Macneil. Those moments made it worthwhile.

Occasionally, someone would find a sexually explicit letter written and unmailed by a now-dead Japanese to his wife at home, reading it aloud for the titillation of all. Frank Tanaka or Lad Nakahara—the team's two wits—could be depended on to say something like, "Well, there's one lady who won't be getting hers anymore."

And the other would respond, "What do you mean, man? She's already getting hers—from the 4-F next door."

The team members were like American GIs in all theaters of combat. They scratched mosquito and other insect bites, complained bitterly about the food—especially the shortage of rice, boasted about their sexual adventures back home, called their commanders dumb—or worse, and dived into foxholes when they heard the dreaded whine of incoming mail.

Their number one complaint was the absence of a different kind of mail. Macneil tried to explain it was probably because the team bounced around so often that their letters from home just had not caught up.

However, a frustrated Corporal Ray Igarashi asked, "Don't you think, Captain Macneil, maybe they're not letting our folks in those relocation centers write to us?"

"I wouldn't put it past the army to do something like that," Macneil replied, "but in this case, I don't think that's the reason. I haven't received any letters myself since getting here four months ago."

That was close enough to the truth, Bill Macneil thought. He did get one letter from his father in October, but he suspected his father, now in Oregon, had pulled strings somewhere to get the missive delivered. The only news of import had been that his sister Sarah was now the protegée of a high-ranking Japanese officer in Shanghai. My God! Macneil thought. What the hell does "protegée" mean? Was she some goddamned Japanese officer's mistress? His sister? Maybe his father had it wrong.

Even if the story was true, Bill knew his kid sister Chankoro too well to accept the story at face value. If she was shacking with someone like that, she had to have an ulterior motive.

Four months in combat had only increased Macneil's dislike of the Japanese. Slats Honda seemed to hold even more hatred for the gooks, as he called them, than his superior. They had both witnessed many Japanese atrocities.

For that reason, it was difficult for Macneil to be too hard on GIs and marines who killed most Japanese prisoners out of hand. One division they had worked with—the 41st, called the "Butcher Division" to distinguish it from the Japanese 41st— made no bones about it: They bragged they "took no prisoners— period."

But Macneil needed prisoners to interrogate, so whenever possible, he talked to the combat troops about the necessity of having *live* Japanese to squeeze intelligence out of. He told them the story of one POW he interrogated who turned out to be code clerk for Lieutenant General Hisao Yamagawa. Within the hour Macneil had radioed this information to ATIS headquarters, and the following day a C-47 flew in and carried the captive code clerk to the code-deciphering outfit at Pearl Harbor.

What brought in more live prisoners than anything else was an inspiration from Slats Honda. He posted a notice on the unit bulletin board:

THREE BOTTLES OF COCA-COLA FOR EVERY LIVE POW.

That did the trick; Coca-Cola was still not being widely distributed to enlisted men. The supply of POWs increased, and so did valuable intelligence.

Because some of the intelligence was important, it had to be disseminated quickly, so ATIS teams were situated as close to the front as possible. There were times when unit commanders ordered Macneil and his men to set their pencils and books aside and pick up their Garands or carbines to reinforce hard-pressed companies.

In Macneil's case, it was a Springfield `03 he grabbed on the run, a more reliable rifle than the new M-1. He knew from experience you could drop it in a swamp and still fire it upon retrieval.

chapter 15

Near Madang, New Guinea
January 1944

Bill Macneil and his ATIS team went into combat again on January 20th. Other American forces were landing on Kwajalein.

"We're being overrun, Macneil," the battalion commander shouted, running up to him. "Get those men of yours into the line—right here," he ordered, stabbing at a map he held.

Macneil summoned his team. "Colonel, you be sure to tell the squads on both sides of us we're American soldiers, understood?"

"All right, all right," the colonel grated, rushing off to muster the cooks and clerks and walking wounded. The situation *was* desperate. The Americans were facing part of the elite Japanese 41st Division commanded by tough, seasoned Major General Adachi.

Two POWs had told Macneil's team that Adachi's men were existing on coconuts and suffering from malnutrition. Also,

Adachi had orders to pull back to Hansa Bay but might risk one last all-out attack with full sound effects before fading into the devilish jungles behind them.

One battalion of the 34th Regiment of the American 24th Infantry Division was drawn up in a line of shallow foxholes behind makeshift barricades. The line extended from the water, across the beach, through a shattered palm grove, and as far as the abruptly rising slopes—covered with seven-foot-high Kunai grass—220 yards from the ocean. Their entrenchments were inadequate but the best they could manage in the time given them.

When Macneil and his eight-member team entered the line under the palm trees at mid-morning, a fierce firefight was underway. The attack had begun at first light. Four full-strength charges by Japanese shock troops had been launched, but still they came on. The Browning light machine guns of the Americans were overheating and would have to have their barrels replaced. Or else.

Another assault began just as Macneil dropped prone behind a palm log and laid out his cartridge belt and bandoleer. The Japanese warriors were shouting as they dashed forward. Their chorus was an odd mixture of English ("Yankee soldier die!" and "Kill Babe Ruth!") and Japanese *"Tenno Heika Banzai!"* ("May the Emperor Reign for Ten Thousand Years!").

But this time, a new twist was being added. Macneil could not believe his ears at first, but the Japanese were singing off-tune and in cracked voices "Deep in the Heart of Texas." Macneil guessed an officer had taught them to sing this in the belief it would make the American audience homesick.

"Fire at will, you people!" Macneil yelled to his team, a totally unnecessary command since the team's rifle and carbine barrels were already hot. Macneil was pushing five-cartridge ammo clips into his bolt-action Springfield, firing as rapidly as he could.

Damn, he thought. They're getting too close. He pulled his Colt .45 1911A1 from its holster and laid it on the log.

The number of dead or wounded in the open space to their front was already so large it was impeding the ability of the attackers to cross the 100 yards dividing the lines. Macneil knew it was going to be a long, hard day. Well, he thought, this is what I signed up for. I've owed these bastards something for a long time and it's payback time. Every time he aimed and squeezed the trigger of his Springfield, he saw not only the Japanese face under that steel helmet plumed with camouflage leaves, but more distant faces from his memory—the soldiers who machine-gunned the Chinese along the banks of the Yangtze and raped the maid in the garden of the Woods' house in Nanking—even the blank faces of those who did something so terrible to Ellen Wood that the girl was still in a mental institution.

This was what Bill Macneil had prayed for, and this was just what he was getting—in full measure. Revenge was sweet, dammit, but how many would he have to kill to quench his thirst?

Despite withering fire from the American battalion, the Japanese—faces distorted in frenzy—came on with magnificent intrepidity. A burning roar filled Macneil's ears and sweat blistered his body. On both flanks machine guns played their threnody. The Japanese were being flung about like bloodied, worn-out toys, but still they came. When they were hit, there was no dramatic outflinging of arms or raising of the face to heaven as movies would have viewers believe. They just collapsed like sacks of potatoes, or like some electrical gadget whose battery has failed.

The survivors of the latest charge withdrew, leaving their dead and dying. A lull followed, and Macneil could hear an insect chirping under the long log protecting his front.

From the Japanese lines an officer in a tropical helmet and kepi charged forth, waving his sword. Screaming *"Banzai! Banzai!"* he ran full tilt toward Macneil's team. By then most of the Americans had hunkered behind whatever protection there was and lit cigarettes or were swigging from their canteens. The enemy officer came on so swiftly and so unexpectedly that those few who saw him could only gape in surprise. Only about 10 yards from Slats Honda, the man skidded to a halt and threw his sword like a spear at the sergeant. It missed. Pulling his Type 14 pistol, he had lurched forward again when Macneil shot him with his .45. That pistol, designed to stop crazed Philippine juramentados in their tracks, broke apart the face of the officer like a melon burst by a baseball bat. He collapsed six feet in front of Macneil. Grinning, Sergeant Honda threw his captain a firm thumbs up.

The American troops had their heads up, nervously alert for what might happen next. They didn't have long to wait. A single Japanese infantryman walked forth from his lines, then stopped and raised both arms. His hands were empty. Macneil knew what the man was up to and started to call a warning down the line, but before he could, an American machine gun on the right flank opened up to smite him. The first burst fell short, but the second caught the Japanese in the back as he turned around. Instantly, a Japanese Type 98 mortar opened up on the machine gun emplacement, destroying it with the second round. The lone Japanese had sacrificed himself so a forward observer could zero in the fire of the 50 mm mortar on the American MG.

Shortly before noon, Japanese Type 92 howitzers began to register, then fire for effect. The barrage grew in volume and intensity. Shells hurtled in, sounding like onrushing freight trains, bracketing the American line. Macneil and his team huddled in their shallow foxholes and behind fallen trees. Concussions shattered the day. The ground throbbed. The cries of the wounded were drowned out. Strangely, one of Macneil's men—Ben Maeda of Honolulu—pulled out his sweet potato and began playing "Manuela Boy." The wavering notes brought a weak laugh from the rest of the team. But the shells kept coming. Coconut palms were uprooted and fell.

Macneil tried to breathe deeply, telling himself he must not break. Over and over he reminded himself: This is what I came for. This is what I came for. Relish the moment, dammit! After 32 endless minutes, the barrage ended. Macneil supposed the howitzer barrels had to be cooled. Then three Bettys flew in low, one after another, and dropped their regards—Macneil guessed they were 100-lb. bombs—on the American positions. They were followed by two Zeros that strafed the line without much effect.

Silence covered the field. The smoke began to drift toward the ocean. "Chow down, boys," Macneil called to his team, reaching for the C-rations from his own pack. He wasn't really hungry, but there was no telling when they would have another respite.

Medics came up at a crouching run to carry the wounded back to the evacuation jeeps. Two ATIS team members were hit. One of them called, "Hey, I'm okay, Captain. I'll get a band-aid and be back in no time." Macneil waved to him. The other wounded man—Corporal Yutaka Sakamoto—was unconscious.

Macneil was pleased to see that the stacks of dead and wounded Japanese were, if anything, higher in front of his section line than on either flank. Let our body count show them whether my men are Americans or not, he thought with savage satisfaction.

Throughout the long, blazing afternoon the fight raged. Ammo and water were brought up; wounded were carried to the rear. By mid-afternoon, when the heat was at its worst, a storm detachment raced from the enemy positions howling with battle lust and rage. Macneil heard the rolling crash of a BAR off to his left.

"Line 'em up and squeeze 'em off, you people!" Bill yelled at his team.

Two American 37 mm guns started scourging the feverishly combative sons of Dai Nihon with canister. Time and again the 37s fired, blowing men to pieces while choking their own crews with fumes from their muzzles. A light tank pulled up behind Macneil's position. When its flame-thrower spewed napalm at the attackers, the fluid did not ignite at first. At least a dozen Japanese had been dowsed with napalm when the tank's machine gunner began firing tracer bullets, igniting the wet Japanese. Once ignited, they danced dervish-like, spinning around and around, drawing a ragged chorus of cheers from the American infantrymen. Dear God, Macneil thought, do we really have to applaud their deaths?

Larger shells began to batter the line. Macneil wondered if the Japanese had anchored a destroyer just off the beach to add the firepower of its six-inch guns. Devastating as these explosives were, they brought one blessing. They scooped out deeper holes in the ground than there had been time to dig.

The other side of the coin became evident at dusk when it

began to rain a torrential downpour measurable in feet, not inches. Every depression filled rapidly. As the water rose, hundreds of crawling creatures from the New Guinea jungle were forced into the open, to float on the water. Among these energetic swimmers were scorpions and vicious white ants, lizards and spiders, snakes—and centipedes so toxic your flesh swelled if they just crawled across your exposed skin.

When at length the downpour stopped, the Japanese celebrated with star shells and parachute flares that bathed the area in ghastly green light. Jillions of mosquitoes shook the water from their wings and formed into attack squadrons, seeming to gain encouragement from the mosquito repellent the GIs rubbed on.

The worst danger from the mosquitoes—even worse than breakbone fever—was that they would sting a man's eyelids so often while he slept that his eyes would be swollen shut when he was awakened—possibly by the sounds of an enemy close at hand.

Three times during the night, Japanese crawled close enough to yell "Gas attack! Gas attack!" in English, but even the greenhorns in the line wouldn't fall for that one anymore. Besides, everyone had thrown away his gas mask and could not have done anything about it, anyway.

The battalion executive officer—a major—crept along the line about two in the morning to prod everyone awake.

"Improve your positions," he kept growling. "Run your wires parallel. Come back for ammo and rations, one or two at a time."

Twenty-five or so feet to his left, Macneil heard someone screaming, then blubbering unintelligibly. The major tried to calm whomever it was but could not. He had to call the medics.

In the morning the mosquitoes were succeeded by flies that

swarmed over the swelling dead at first light.

All the men, Macneil included, were desperate for sleep, but if they collapsed from weariness now and if the Japanese attacked again—still, their enemies were only human and they needed sleep too.

Many Americans, of course, refused to grant that the Japanese were human at all. Instead, they were beasts to be exterminated like plague-bearing rats. Or they were incredibly hardy jungle fighters who were born and raised in an environment like New Guinea's.

Macneil smiled to himself when he thought of the gross misconceptions each side had of the other. He had once tried to tell three infantrymen of the 24th Division that Japan was not really a land of torrid, snaky jungles and swamps.

"But then how did they learn to fight in this terrain the way they do, Captain?" one of the men—from Iowa—asked, moving his tobacco cud to the right side of his jaw.

"They learned the same damned way you're learning, soldier," Macneil replied. "The hard way."

The light tank of yesterday afternoon had its flamethrower working. With two more tanks in support, the first shouldered through the line and onto the killing field. The treads of all three crushed and mangled the Japanese dead and wounded. From the rear the treads resembled meat grinders.

The tanks forced the Japanese to retreat. In less than an hour the enemy had gone and the field was silent. Cautiously, the Americans climbed out of their water-filled holes to dry out—and catch whatever sleep they could before something else happened.

That afternoon some of the men roused themselves enough to stagger down to the beach for a saltwater bath. Bill Macneil walked out in front to view the aftermath. He estimated more than 500 dead. The bodies were just beginning to smell. How fast we mortals putrefy, he thought.

All the helmets bore the star of the Japanese army. Heads lolled, mouths agape. Teeth shone white in bloodstained, smoke-blackened faces. These inscrutable dead had looked up that morning at the rising sun with glazed, unseeing eyes. Some were cut in two by machine-gun bursts. Strangely, one man had his head forced down in his chest so it was only half visible. Another had the top of his skull blown off neatly, the cavity filled with rainwater. "The shithead," commented Slats Honda who was walking just behind his captain. Indifferently, he flipped a pebble into the cavity.

Macneil wondered why Slats Honda hated the Japanese so much. He and the sergeant would have to exchange stories some day.

Most of the Japanese lay in the grotesque positions of sudden death. Nothing stays so quiet and still as a dead soldier, Macneil thought. These boys had given their all for the emperor. Macneil turned aside. He could not push away a compulsion to feel sorry for them. He could see the wrinkled, sunburned faces of old women in rural farmhouses in Japan, dreading word that their son or grandson had gone to his eternal rest in Yasukuni Shrine. Their sorrow would be real, just as real as the suffering of these young men at his feet had been. He wanted to hate these dead, but had any of them been at Nanking?

"Let's get out of here, Slats."

"Right behind you, Captain."

Slouched and dragging their weapons in the wet sand, the ATIS team slowly made its way to the bivouac. After arranging their mosquito nets, they collapsed, completely exhausted.

Macneil slumped down to write a radio message requesting replacement for the wounded Sakamoto. Slats Honda stayed with Bill to carry the message to the communications tent. While waiting, the sergeant turned on the radio owned by the team and spun the dial until he found a woman's voice speaking in English.

"Here she is," he said happily to Macneil. "She's what I've been waiting for."

Distracted, Macneil looked up from the message form. "Who's that?"

"You know, Captain. That dame outta Tokyo. That announcer, Orphan Annie. You've heard her, haven't you?"

"Seems to me I've heard you men talking about her."

A recording of "Strike Up the Band" ended and then the woman spoke. "Hello there, fellows. How's tricks? Guess who? None other than your own Annie. Miss me? It's been a week. I've been hearing a nasty rumor you guys like my music more than me. Can that be true? Well, in just a minute I'll play for you something better than Ketelbey's 'In a Persian Garden,' all right? But first I've got some news for you from home. Not good news, I'm afraid. They're rioting in Detroit again. Sixteen Negroes killed and—"

Macneil dropped his pencil. "I think I know that voice."

"No shit? You know this gal?"

"Jeepers, fellows," the female voice went on, "things sure do sound bad in Detroit. I hope none of your folks are around there right now. Anyway, it's time for our musical interlude. This time your playmate Orphan Annie wants to let you listen to 'I'm in the Mood for Love,' played by Artie Shaw and his orchestra. Don't you wish you were home about to take your girl out dancing? Well, leaping lizards, do I ever know how you feel! Do I ever! So

I'll play this number for Tom and Art and especially for you, Bill. Sweet dreams and love from your bitter enemy in Tokyo."

"Yeah, Slats. I guess I do," Macneil said musingly, handing Sergeant Honda the radio message.

Only there was no guesswork. Macneil did know that voice. One hundred and ten percent certain. The song she selected. Her way of dropping and slightly drawing out the last word of every sentence. She even worked in his name. It was Helma Graf, all right.

When Bill Macneil lay down, he fully expected to sleep the slumber of the dead. He had never gone through a day like this one. No—not even that first day in Nanking when he and Ellen Wood's family were so desperately searching for her. Here he had been in the line since mid-morning. He had killed men beyond counting. His emotions had run the gamut from battle lust through fear to grim satisfaction, but now he felt totally drained of emotion. His sleep would be, he thought, no more than blank unconsciousness.

But that was not to be. Instead, he dreamed of Helma Graf in disconnected segments. He held open his arms to her, but Helma rejected him, turning away to wrap herself in a Rising Sun flag. Then he dreamed he had just married her, but when she lifted her wedding veil for a nuptial kiss, he found himself face to face with the poster caricature of a Jap soldier's features, buck teeth, slanted eyes and all. Next, they were on a dance floor, and he wanted to dance the tango with her, but she kept slipping out of his arms to dance with Japanese men.

When Slats Honda roused him the next morning, Bill Macneil was just as tired as he had been the night before.

chapter 16

Outside Wewak, New Guinea
May 1944

MacArthur continued to fight his way along the formidable North Coast of New Guinea.

His tactics included converging, leap-frogging, and pincer attacks. By April, he had forced the Japanese as far back as Wewak, where their 18th Army with 51,000 troops was dug in behind strong defensive positions.

Douglas MacArthur calculated the cost of a head-on assault on Wewak, then considered the alternatives. He had the Army's 40th Infantry Division, as well as elements of the 6th and the 32nd, ready to bypass Wewak—to let it wither on the vine, in one of his favorite locutions—but a principal concern was not to overextend and leave his forces vulnerable to a flank attack.

Wewak and its vicinity were well within range of the 5th Air Force led by the feisty General George Kenney, but so far Kenney's recon flights had come up with scant tactical intelligence on the strength of Japanese forces on the Admiralty Islands across from New Guinea. In particular, Manus Island had caught MacArthur's worried eye. He was certain Japanese units were there, well concealed in dugouts, caves, and under dense jungle foliage. But he needed to know their strength, their unit designations, and whether those troops were more of the crack forces transferred from China or merely old men and young boys recently drafted back in Japan.

The ATIS team members were still chiding Bill Macneil about his "girl friend" at Radio Tokyo. No disclaimer from him made any difference. His team had sunk its teeth into this rumor and gnawed happily away on it.

"Say, Captain, did you listen to your girl friend last night?"

"What's she look like, sir?"

"How about showing us a picture?"

"Where did she get a name like Little Orphan Annie?"

Macneil took their ribbing in good spirit. "Do you really like her voice? I thought Tokyo Rose would be more your type."

"Hell, no . . . sir. I like those soft, feminine voices."

The officers from the unit the ATIS team was temporarily assigned to were blunter and more intrusive. "Hey, Macneil, I hear you got a little Nip girl friend on Radio Tokyo."

Stung, Macneil turned on one infantry captain. "Listen, you son of a bitch. The woman you're talking about is a Caucasian. She's a Swiss neutral. And she's not my girl friend. I had a couple of dates with her in the summer of 1941, that's all. And I'm not even sure this so-called Little Orphan Annie is the same person."

From the paratrooper's stance, the infantry captain must have sensed he was ready to fight. "Don't get your bowels in an uproar, Bill." He raised his open palms. "They've got so many announcers on that station I can't tell one from another. Except that one with the kinda funny voice—Tokyo Rose."

As the regiment made its tortuous way through the coastal jungle toward Wewak, the Japanese gave way stubbornly, fiercely resisting. A few Japanese prisoners were taken and interrogated. Documents were examined and translated in full on the spot or marked for later translation in Australia. An entire squad of the 3rd Battalion was ambushed by the Japanese at a river crossing and captured or killed, their bodies thrown in the river to be washed into the sea.

The Americans continued their steady advance, until they came upon the bodies of three men from the missing squad. One corpse was left along a dim trail, its stench detectable at 75 yards. A second had been strung up against a tree trunk and evidently used for bayonet practice, judging from countless stabbing wounds.

The third corpse was most revolting. Dozens of Americans shoved through the tall cogen grass to see if the rumor was true and to curse the Japanese, "Every god-damned one of 'em." Macneil, while ashamed of his curiosity, went forward with the others.

His hands tied behind him, the putrefying American soldier was leaning back against a tree trunk, facing the direction from which his comrades were sure to come. His decapitated head sat on his lap. The man's genitalia—or what was left of them—were stuffed into his mouth. This genital mutilation must have been done after death, for there was little blood showing on the leaves below the crotch. At least he had been spared that.

Word of the atrocities spread through the regiment like a prairie fire on the plains of Kansas. Of course, there had been other incidents of extreme cruelty by the Japanese, but this one seemed to take a prize for deep-dyed evil.

Then came an even more nauseating report: Hungry Japanese soldiers had begun to practice cannibalism on prisoners, an exercise they called "living meat." Prisoners were tied to trees and fillets of flesh were cut from their thighs or buttocks. Damp pandanus leaves were plastered against the wounds to ward off flies and prevent infestation by maggots. Prisoners could be kept alive for even a week while they continued to provide fresh meat for their captors.

This gruesome tale made the rounds of the regiment in a single day. By the next morning, the GIs were begging the colonel to let them drive ahead immediately. Everyone had an unholy blood lust in his eyes and fulsome curses on his lips.

The only problem was, the story was totally false. Some thoughtless noncombatant from a quartermaster unit had delivered the tale along with frozen food from a supply ship.

He had heard the story from a missionary, who told the quartermaster the practice of "living meat" could be traced to a tribe called the Orokaivas ("Spear Men") of many years ago. The quartermaster youngster had merely substituted "Japs" for "Orokaivas" and earned himself a large audience only too ready to believe anything wicked about their despised enemy.

What the Japanese had actually done was bad enough, Macneil thought, and did not need to be embellished or exaggerated. Still, these atrocities puzzled him. He knew the Combatants' Code (*Senjinkun*) of the Japanese army well enough. Every soldier was required to carry a copy in his uniform pocket. Macneil had translated the code and remembered one of its admonitions: "If you pretend to be valorous," the emperor had warned, "but act with unseemly violence, the world will regard you as a wild beast. You should not stain the Imperial honor by atrocious behavior."

Every Japanese in uniform knew those words as well as Americans knew the pledge of allegiance, so why did they commit such sickening acts?

Macneil had not been raised in a military tradition, but he knew that professional military men of the Western world—while accepting the necessity of war—had a certain respect for an enemy and recognized duty as duty, bravery as bravery, fortitude as fortitude, whether in friend or foe. He knew in his heart that many Japanese officers abided by the highest standards of conduct. These were not men like those who had countenanced the Rape of Nanking, but more like General Kiyotake Kawaguchi, whose profile Bill had read in a military intelligence study entitled "Know Your Enemy." Kawaguchi had worked in a POW camp in World War I and was known for his humane treatment of German prisoners under his care. In the present war he had defied Imperial General Headquarters by refusing to condone revenge killings of senior Philippine officials. To kill an enemy in cold blood, he held, was a violation of the Code of Bushido. Dispatched to retake Guadalcanal, Kawaguchi had led two attacks on Bloody Ridge that were foredoomed to be turned back. Refusing to sacrifice any more of his men in futile assaults, Kawaguchi withdrew and later chastised the general staff for ordering him to take a strong enemy position with a night attack. (He pointed out that even a recruit would know better.) He was relieved of command and his successor ordered to resume the offensive against Bloody Ridge, where the attacking Japanese forces were obliterated.

General Masafumi Yamauchi was a gentle, frail man who had

been a military attaché in Washington and earned a certain reputation by carrying a Western-style latrine with him on campaigns. (His only food was oatmeal, milk, and fresh-baked bread.) He treated with such kind consideration the Burmese through whose country his army marched that eventually his superior, General Renya Mutaguchi, had Yamauchi and his staff packed off to the rear.

Perhaps such Japanese generals were few in number, but Macneil knew they were not entirely nonexistent. How to explain cruelty and decency living side by side? What happened that made one man become a monster while the next became a saint? In Nanking, the general commanding Japanese forces in Central China—Iwane Matsui—had come to the city from his headquarters in Shanghai shortly after its capture. He had heard disturbing reports about the raping and pillaging of his troops and set out to inspect the city and bring the atrocities to an end. But his superior, Prince Asaka—the emperor's uncle, prevented Matsui from seeing too much of the savage barbarity and had him ushered by riverboat back to his Shanghai headquarters. Evil had conquered good.

Macneil had often debated this anomaly with fellow officers and with members of his ATIS team. Back in their home islands, Japanese were among the best behaved people in the world, but in other countries Japanese soldiers sometimes became ravening beasts. Obviously, the social controls exerted on them in Japan did not export well, but why would not their officers perform the restraining role played by society back home?

Was it because the Japanese looked upon other Asians as creatures beneath their contempt? Did their long-standing resentment of arrogant white men in Asia at last boil over and madden them with a satanic thirst for retribution? Did their samurai belief that courageous warriors never surrendered render them incapable of treating American prisoners like other—if lesser— human beings? Macneil did not know and would not pretend he did. But the questions vexed him.

Part of the answer, Macneil reflected, might be found in one sentence he recalled reading in a Japanese army training manual. It warned "those becoming prisoners of war will suffer the death penalty at the hands of the enemy." In black and white. "If they take you alive, they'll kill you." If you believed that—and what Japanese enlisted man did not believe an army manual?—then you need have no compunction about killing enemy prisoners out of hand. They were going to do the same to you, weren't they?

There was also the widely misunderstood Geneva Convention. Macneil had never spoken to an American in uniform who did not assume the Japanese were bound by the provisions of the convention regarding treatment of prisoners, but it was not so. Japan had never ratified the Geneva provisions.

The reason for Japan's failure was simple: Japan was afraid her soldiers and sailors would interpret decent treatment of Allied prisoners as condoning their own surrender. The American military never thought to question the matter. The United States was a signatory to the convention, so it was to be assumed all belligerents were bound by its provisions. Japan was not.

Macneil would have hated to be a lawyer in a courtroom arguing either side of the case. There was so much hatred and incomprehension on both sides that clear, dispassionate thinking was well-nigh impossible. He doubted there had ever been an enemy of Americans—with the possible exception of certain Indian tribes—as deeply despised as the Japanese in this conflict.

If only they would not do such terrible things as the mutilating of the American POW Macneil had just seen on the jungle trail. And, of course, whatever literally unspeakable acts they had committed against the innocent person of Ellen Wood in Nanking.

Macneil was no sooner back at the ATIS tents from viewing the atrocity on the jungle trail than he received a summons to report on the double to the regimental commander. Thirty minutes later he came hurrying back at a half-run and pulled Slats Honda aside.

"We've got us one hell of a mission, Slats."

"Us, Captain?"

"You and I are going to parachute on to Manus Island tonight."

"Sweet Mother of Jesus, Captain. Why me? I've never parachuted anywhere. . . ."

"I'll teach you everything you need to know by tonight."

The sergeant was not short on courage, but he quailed at the thought of a parachute drop into an enemy jungle. "Have a heart, Captain Macneil. There must be some other people who have jumped in this regiment."

"I'm sure there are, but none of them speak Japanese. No, Slats, don't argue about it. Our orders are clear. Two ATIS personnel must be dropped tonight by parachute on Manus. MacArthur wants to know who's on the island and he wants to know in one hell of a hurry."

"Captain, I've never told you this, but I get fainting spells at heights over fifty feet."

"Cut the crap, Sergeant. Let's get the lead out."

The red light over the door to the pilot's compartment came

on. The air force lieutenant at the controls had been groaning almost since reaching flying altitude. He had eaten beans, rice, and hash for dinner and was suffering excruciating gas pains.

The navigator yelled, "Four minutes!"

Bill Macneil and Slats Honda stood up to buckle the two groin straps of their chute harnesses, then secured the third strap across their chests.

"Jesus, Bill," Honda complained, addressing him without a title for the first time. "I'm scared shitless. Do I really have to do this?"

Macneil slapped his sergeant on the back. "Piece of cake, Slats. Don't sweat it." Macneil could not tell Honda that he was nervous, too. He always was when jumping. Although there was that tremendous exultation the jumper felt when his chute snapped open, he could not totally ignore the small voice within that kept chanting, "What if the damned chute doesn't open? What if the damned chute doesn't open? What if the damned—"

That was why they each had two chutes—no, really three: the backpack main chute, the chestpack reserve, and inside the latter a small pilot chute, only 30 inches in diameter, compared to the twenty-eight-foot canopy of the main chute.

The C-47—known by all who loved her as a Gooney Bird—descended rapidly in the darkness of the moonless night. The aircraft was black—the same color as the silk of the chutes. Even their twenty-eight shroud lines were black. Everything was black, including the bottomless emptiness below. The pilot's only aiming point was the white of the phosphorescent surf breaking on the beach along the north shore of Manus. They were jumping from 500 feet, which meant almost no margin.

Macneil hooked his static line to the anchor cable overhead

and motioned for Honda to do the same. The sergeant crossed himself.

"I didn't know you were a Catholic."

"I'm not. I'm just pushing all buttons."

"You go first."

"After you. Rank has its privileges."

"If I go first, you might forget to follow—so get your ass up here." Macneil pulled the large bundle behind him toward the exit and hooked its line to the anchor cable. It was the inflatable rubber raft they planned to use two days later when a PT boat was slated to meet them 300 yards off shore.

The green light flashed. Macneil gave Honda an encouraging shove. Next to go was the rubber raft, then Macneil.

Both Americans were carrying more than 100 pounds of equipment, adding to the shock they felt in the crotch and armpits when their chutes popped and billowed above them.

Macneil pulled his risers to direct his landing to the beach. Assuming the fetal position, he braced himself for the landing and hoped Honda was doing the same. The soft sand and his bent legs absorbed the shock. Quickly, he spilled the air from his parachute and slipped out of the harness. While looking for Honda and the raft, he unholstered his pistol.

The raft had landed in the surf so Macneil ran to retrieve it before it was washed away. Then he saw a flashlight beam moving back and forth beneath palms lining the beach. He hoped it was Honda and that the sergeant had landed unhurt. Before going to check, Macneil dug a hole in the sand with his entrenching tool, burying his black parachute and the shovel. With his hands he scooped sand into the hole. Then he dragged the raft into the shelter of the palms.

He paused to listen and to look. The flashlight beam still moved back and forth. A mild wind rustled the palm fronds. Waves lapped at the beach fifteen yards away. All else was stillness and darkness. So far, so good. Now to get his sergeant and move away from the drop area, in case a suspicious patrol had heard the Gooney Bird and decided to investigate. After all, seldom did aircraft fly that low in the middle of the night.

Honda's parachute had caught in the top of a palm tree, and the sergeant had dangled from his shroud lines until he twisted and turned to cut himself loose. Macneil calculated he must have fallen at least fifteen feet.

"It's a wonder you didn't break something," Macneil said, lifting the Nisei to his feet.

"I almost wish I had. Then maybe you wouldn't take me along on any more of your fun-filled picnics."

Macneil ignored him and looked toward the top of the tree. "We haven't got time to haul that chute down. We'll have to take a chance and leave it up there."

"If it's the chute you're so worried about, Captain, I'll just stay here and guard it till you get back from your little stroll through this jungle—which, by the way, smells even worse than those on New Guinea."

"Decaying vegetation, Slats. Mount up. We want to be a couple of miles away from here by first light."

"Walk through this shit at night, Captain? Have you lost your mind?"

"Stay here if you like," Macneil said, starting to push through the vegetation toward the center of the island. He heard the sounds of the sergeant coming along, as he knew he would.

Where they slept that night they had not the faintest notion.

Wherever it was, it was dark and damp and stank evilly. They pulled leaves and grass over themselves to ward off mosquitoes and, they hoped, other bugs. It did not take Macneil long to fall asleep, but during the short time he was still awake, he was forced to listen to the lonely, cruel sounds of jungle night life. Somewhere near at hand a snake—he supposed it was a snake—had caught a frog—he supposed it was a frog—and was leisurely savoring its midnight snack. The frog's piteous croaks slowly decreased in volume and frequency and at last descended into oblivion.

At first light, Macneil shook his sergeant awake.

"I was dreaming I was back in Fresno," Honda grumbled.

"With your family?"

"Well, at least the part of it I care anything about."

"Let's open a can of hash and be on our way. We've only got until tomorrow night."

The going grew easier as they climbed toward the center of Manus. By noon they were at an altitude that allowed them to see what appeared to be two Japanese encampments. Most of the enemy huts and tents were beneath foliage, so Macneil could not estimate the strength of whatever unit was stationed there. Getting closer would be tricky, so their best course was to capture and question one or more of the enemy.

By the end of the first day, they had spotted a third encampment on the western end of Manus but had not come close to any soldiers. Again that night they slept under leaves on the jungle floor.

Shortly after noon the next day, their luck changed. Two Japanese came walking toward them on a jungle trail. They were laughing and talking about something they had done with a pair of comfort girls the night before.

"Comfort girls?" Honda had whispered. "On this island?"

"Shut up." Macneil drew his Colt automatic. "Wait till they get abreast of us. I'll take the one in front."

When the two Japanese were bound and half-shoved, half-carried deeper into the tropical growth, Macneil let them sit down and removed the gags from their mouths while holding the muzzle of his automatic within a foot of their faces.

Macneil and Honda had an interrogation routine they had perfected and used many times. Honda took one of the captives farther off and began to talk to him as Macneil did with the other. At first, the two Japanese were sullen and totally unresponsive, but then Macneil and Honda traded places. That seemed to disorient the enemy. First, why was a man with a Japanese face wearing an American uniform? Second, who was the hairy barbarian who spoke better Japanese than the fellow with the Japanese face?

Both men accepted American cigarettes and that relaxed them to a degree, although neither Macneil nor Honda liked the idea of smoke curling upwards through the vegetation.

The same questions were repeated over and over. What unit? What battalion? What regiment? What's the strength of your regiment? When did you reach Manus? Where did you come from? What other units are on this island? What's the total strength?

Piece by piece information was elicited. The prisoners mentioned their hometowns. Macneil had never visited either of them but knew enough about Japan—after all, it was his home—to sound as if he did.

Did you get down to the beach often? (Very few towns in Japan were far from the ocean.) Do those "sellers of spring" (*baishumpu*) still gather around the train station in the early evening? (The stations were where you could find the whores in any town.) I wonder how the cherry blossoms were this year? I know your town is famous for them. (Most Japanese towns are inordinately proud of the beauty of their cherry trees in bloom.) I went swimming once in the river that runs through the town. What was the name of it? (All towns had rivers flowing through them.)

Bit by bit the two captives dropped their guard and became, if not friendly, at least less hostile and a little more open.

Honda and Macneil followed their customary practice of playing one off against the other. "You say you're attached to the 22nd Division? Private Watanabe just told the sergeant over there your division is the 28th." "Three thousand men in your camp? It doesn't look that big. I'll go over and take a closer look tonight. You might as well tell us the truth. We'll find out anyway." And so on.

Eventually, they got what they needed. They would report there were in excess of 8,000 troops on Manus, in three encampments. Three batteries of Type 94 mountain guns, 75mm. One battery of 37 mm Type 1 antitank guns. All part of the 28th. No tanks. Rumors were rife that Manus would soon be evacuated and the troops withdrawn to Rabaul.

The sun was westering. They still had to make their way through the heavy undergrowth to the coast while it was light. Bringing the two prisoners together, Macneil tied the arms of both behind their backs, then bound their feet. Eventually, they would work themselves free and go running back to camp, although in their shame at being captured, there was no telling what they might report to their CO.

Macneil and Honda started north at a half-run, but before

they had gone fifty yards, the sergeant stopped and said, "I forgot something. Don't wait for me. I'll catch up."

But the ATIS captain did wait—in a turmoil of indecision. He knew why Slats Honda had gone back. He knew what he was going to do just as sure as he knew the sun above them was going to set in a little more than an hour.

He told himself he should go back and stop the sergeant but he hesitated—until it was too late.

chapter 17

The PT boat pickup went off without a hitch.

Back at the base, Macneil and Honda reverted to their daily routine of translation and occasional interrogations. The ATIS captain still had not confronted his sergeant with direct questions about what he suspected had taken place on Manus. That time would come, Macneil thought. In any event, there was nothing to be done about it. If Slats really had killed the two Japanese prisoners, he could justify the act by pleading self-preservation. Had the prisoners worked themselves free of their bonds, they would have raised an alarm and 8,000 Japanese soldiers might have fanned out over Manus in a massive manhunt. Besides, Macneil could not clear his memory of the dead American with his head in his lap and his genitals in his mouth.

Despite his pent-up animosity toward the Japanese, Macneil

did not believe he could bring himself to do what he suspected Slats Honda had done. Such an act was abominable and barbaric. Even if an enemy did such things or worse, he was far from certain he could do them himself.

Smiling to himself, he reflected on how much Helma Graf would have loved to hear such sentiments. Love your fellow man, ran her constant message. Have compassion. Try to understand. Turn the other cheek. Never cut the throat of a prisoner just to insure his silence.

Two days later, Macneil was seated at a table in the ATIS tent reviewing a translation when a Nisei corporal—a stranger—lifted a flap.

"Captain Macneil?" The man came to attention and saluted. "Corporal Sidney Furuiye reporting for duty, sir. ATIS sent me up from Australia." He placed his orders on the table in front of Macneil.

The corporal was slightly overweight, short, and dressed in battle fatigues. He had a fiery red scar on the right side of his neck. His face was round with alert narrow eyes. There was humor in his face, and he seemed to be on the point of smiling.

"Sit down, Corporal."

Macneil interviewed the new addition to his team, first in English and then in Japanese. Furuiye—he liked to be called Sid, he said—had never been in Japan, but his immigrant parents, from Hiroshima, had always spoken Japanese at home and had sent both their children to a Japanese language school in Honolulu that conducted classes for two hours in the late afternoon.

Macneil decided Sid was as competent as the rest of the ATIS team, with the exception of Slats Honda. He explained the routine and said the sergeant would help him get settled in.

"There's one other thing, Sid, that I want to talk to you about. It's a little lecture I give to replacements. Not about our work here in these tents but about combat in these jungles."

"Combat, Captain?" Furuiye sat forward in his chair. "I mean . . . well, I thought this was . . . uh, like a desk job, you know?"

"That's what it's supposed to be, but now and then we get shoved into the lines. It happened just the other day. I'm sure the boys will tell you all about it. And that's why you're here. You are replacing Yutaka Sakamoto, who was wounded. By the way, did you hear how he's doing?"

Sid Furuiye shook his head.

"Anyway, it will happen again—the combat, I mean—and that's what I want to talk about."

The new man nodded, but Macneil wondered if he was really ready to absorb what he was about to say. You can tell some people the same thing a dozen times over, but they won't take it to heart until they have an experience that proves it.

"Is it always this hot here, Captain?"

"I'm afraid it is, but now I want you to listen. First thing to remember when you are on the line is how vital it is to be silent. Absolute quiet. Learn to communicate by signals and gestures. Wrap everything you carry in paper or rags to absorb sound. Even your dog tags. We pick up Japanese gas masks and cut up the rubber tubing to rim our dog tags. And get someone to show you the right way to dig a foxhole. We always dig deeper pockets in the four corners so if a grenade is tossed in, we can kick it into one of those corner holes to lessen the effect of the blast." Macneil could see that he was beginning to hold the young fellow's attention.

145

"Next, always carry a large nail with you. You can use it to pound a hole in a coconut and get a drink when you think you're dying of thirst out there. Then, remember the best Japanese weapon is the Nambu light machine gun. For some reason, they always fire it in bursts of six to eight rounds. It's not easy, but try to count the rounds. After six or so, you know you have a breather of about ten seconds to run to a dugout or the next hole. Don't forget booby traps. I'm sure you've been told this over and over, but never pick up anything from the field. They'll even booby-trap the body of a dead American. You can figure there'll be a sniper in every other tree. Count on it and watch for them. Keep your weapon clean. The infantry sergeants will tell you that till they're blue in the face, but it really is important. That's why I carry a Springfield `03. It doesn't jam the way a Garand does. At night, if they think they've gotten some dirt down the barrel, some fellows even drop fireflies down there to check." Macneil paused to drink from his canteen.

"Oh yeah, remember the Japanese like to attack on com- memorative days—their national holidays. All you men know what days those are: the emperor's birthday, Boys' Day, and so forth. And don't be fooled by any calls or cries in English you hear at night. Chances are it'll be the enemy. A few of them speak pret- ty good English, as you must know. Put shoe polish, if you have any, on any piece of equipment that shines. If you're near the beach, listen for the sound of beach wash that is different from the sound of the surf. Beach wash will tell you that a boat— maybe an enemy boat—is running along parallel to the beach at high speed. If a barrage is coming in, keep your head down if you're in a hole. That's obvious. If you're on flat ground, try to crawl away from a rocky area. A shell exploding on rock will break it into splinters that are as bad as shrapnel. Learn about insects: which are poisonous and which ones aren't. If you're ever wounded and can't get quick first aid, remember a maggot is your best friend. I know that's a hell of a thing to say, but if you find maggots in your wound, leave them there. They're eating at the infection and will leave the wound as clean as a whistle."

Macneil paused to catch his breath. He nodded his permission for the new man to smoke.

"If you're in the line at night and hear your own wounded calling out, remember that those men who are crying for their mothers are likely to be the ones closest to death. But, if they're cursing Douglas MacArthur or Hirohito or President Roosevelt, then they're probably still in fair to middling shape."

Furuiye finished his cigarette.

"That's enough for today," Macneil told him. "Go see Sergeant Honda and let him get you squared away."

The replacement stood and saluted.

"We don't salute inside these tents . . . or outside," Macneil said. "The more I get saluted, the better chance I have a sniper will scope in on me." Macneil shook the new man's hand. "I'm glad to have you here. I think you'll do all right. If you've got problems, talk to Sergeant Honda first, then come to see me if you want to."

Later, Bill Macneil reflected on the advice he had given Furuiye. There was more he could have said and, without doubt, would have occasion to say in the future, but the new people could only absorb so much.

He had not gotten around to probably the most important advice, which was why soldiers fight. If Macneil had learned anything in New Guinea, it was that military men don't fight for home and country and family. The patriotic rhetoric was all about "God and honor and native land," and a lot of American GIs and marines would pay lip service to those ideals, but what they were really fighting for was each other. They fought not for flag or glory or Mom's apple pie or hamburgers, but for the brotherhood of battle, for that mysterious fraternity born in the closeness of death. Their loyalty to the buddy in the next foxhole transcended all. The sacrifices they would make for each other were astounding. Over and over they risked their lives for their comrades. That was what wise leaders always strove to foster in their troops: the unity and cohesiveness arising from shared danger. Macneil hoped Sidney Furuiye would learn that, too, with all else he needed to know.

That evening, three members of the ATIS team were working late in the second team tent. Macneil walked over to see how they were doing. The regiment had advanced up the coast nearly two miles and had brought in more maps, diaries, and documents than usual. What the team could not review in the next couple of days would have to be sent back to ATIS in Australia.

The shortwave radio sat on one of the work tables and was turned on at low volume. A woman, not Helma Graf, was announcing the news from Radio Tokyo. Macneil thought she was the one known among the Americans as Tokyo Rose.

"News has been received of the sinking of a Japanese hospital ship, the *Buenos Aires-maru*, by four B-17 bombers of the American air force. This vessel had large Red Cross signs painted on both sides. It sank in thirty minutes. This happened off the coast of Taiwan. A surviving nurse, Tome Sasajima, who was in a lifeboat, has reported that the Americans strafed the survivors 'like some fearful birds of prey, raining machine gun fire on us.'"

The ATIS men, with Bill Macneil, listened in silence to the news.

Gary Morimoto threw down his pencil. "I don't believe Americans would do anything like that."

"Naw, that's just propaganda, man," Frank Tanaka said in agreement.

Bill Macneil nodded, too, but in his heart he wondered. The Radio Tokyo people had beamed many half-truths and out-and-out lies toward the South Pacific, but somehow he wondered if this report might not be true.

He had seen American men in uniform do things of late he would never before have believed. Some of these callous acts were so shocking he had tried to obliterate them from his mind, to pretend he had not seen them, but the memories would not fade.

He had watched a two-man flamethrower team adjust the stream of fire from their weapon so it did not kill their Japanese targets instantly but let them linger in agony. Once he had seen a GI slit open the cheek of a wounded Japanese—still conscious— to prize out his gold-crowned teeth with a bayonet.

The worst was an American first lieutenant who was with the regiment the ATIS team had joined in April. Whenever this officer found a dead Japanese on the battlefield, he would force open the mouth of the corpse and urinate in it.

The Japanese stuffing a dead American's genitals into his mouth and Americans pissing in the mouths of Japanese corpses set Bill Macneil to thinking of the words of an old Negro spiritual: "Ain't gwine to study war no more."

CHAPTER 18

Tokyo, Japan
October 1944

Douglas MacArthur kept his promise to the people of the Philippines. At the head of his army, he had waded through the surf of a Leyte beach and returned to the Philippines to drive out the Japanese. In his grandiose rhetoric, the commander of Allied forces in the southwest Pacific called on the Filipinos to rise and throw off the yoke of the invaders from the north.

Japanese rhetoric—at least, what the government announced for the ears of the public—did not suffer from comparison with that of Douglas MacArthur. If anything, MacArthur's pronouncements were not quite as vainglorious as those of his enemy. Japanese communiqués made extensive use of pompous self-glorification. Their airmen became "wild eagles," and when it had to be admitted one of them was shot down by the foe, his aircraft was reported as being "self-destroyed," with the clear implication that the pilot—the "wild eagle"—had deliberately crashed into the deck of an American warship. The Imperial Navy was always called the "invincible navy." Those killed in combat became "hero-gods" to be forever honored in the Yasukuni Shrine in Tokyo. The people themselves constituted the "rear front" or the "Hundred Million," although the population of the country was only 74,000,000—and fast declining. Many did not swallow this nonsense, but who had the courage to call the hand of the military propagandists?

Helma Graf knew the dismal truth because she read the transcripts of American shortwave broadcasts, as monitored by Kyodo, and she was saddened. Not because Japan was being soundly defeated, but because the war was still going on at all, because men on both sides were still dying by the tens of thousands. The more she prayed for peace and universal love, the more the hatreds seemed to deepen, the more desperate the fighting grew.

Life in the Macneil mansion in Azabu continued on a descending level of comfort. With so much privation and hunger around them, there was little time for the residents to enjoy the marvelous October weather.

Shipton Macneil had turned eighteen the previous month, precipitating a crisis of decision. He had to decide whether to continue to be an American, as he had always regarded himself, or to take Japanese citizenship. If he opted to retain his American identity—and his treasured passport, he became an adult enemy alien, whereas until now, he had been merely a minor enemy alien, regarded as relatively harmless by the authorities.

As an adult enemy alien, however, Shipton would be reclassified and interned elsewhere in Japan. If it had been possible, he would have been deported, but no more repatriation vessels were sailing from Japanese ports. And there was no way the authorities would allow him to remain where he was, any more than Japanese aliens were permitted to move about freely or reside wherever they pleased in the United States.

If he chose to become a Japanese citizen, he would, of course, be allowed to remain with, and provide care and protection for, his invalid mother.

"Don't give up your citizenship, Ship," Helma had pleaded with him.

"But don't you see? I must stay with Mother. She can hardly move about, Helma. How could I just abandon her to—"

"I'm here, aren't I? I promise you I'll care for her like my own mother, Ship. Believe me. After all, some day, when Bill and I—" She stopped in embarrassment.

Ship Macneil shook his head miserably. "I know you would do your best, but I've sworn to stay at Mother's side as long as she needs someone to care for her. I appreciate your willingness—I really do, Helma—but this is something I have to do. The Americans will start bombing Tokyo soon—that's the rumor—and I'll have to be here to do something—maybe take Mother out into the country, maybe even to our old place down in Nagasaki."

Even taking Japanese citizenship was not entirely a "before-breakfast chore," as the Japanese would say. To become natural-ized, Shipton had to apply to the *Homusho*, the Ministry of Justice, and report for an interview to determine his *doka-sei*: his assimilability. The interviewing official wanted to gauge his knowledge of Japan and the Japanese language and to judge his capacity for adapting to, what the official called, the *Nihonjin no seikatsu yoshiki* or Japanese style of living.

In the case of Shipton Macneil, of course, that did not present a problem. He was half-Japanese. His Japanese was as good as his English. And when the Ministry of Justice learned, somewhat to their surprise, that he was the grandson of ex-Ambassador Tomoji Miyoshi, now a senior advisor to the Ministry of Foreign Affairs, they practically fell over themselves to approve his application and to list him in the Miyoshi family register. The local draft board was also informed that another human being was now available as grist for the mills of war.

In his new documentation, Shipton Macneil was listed as Wataru (a name of his own choosing) Miyoshi. He was entered on the rolls of the *tonari-gumi,* or neighborhood association, as an adult resident and would henceforth be called on to train for, and engage in, such cooperative activities as fire fighting, filling emergency water reservoirs, and spreading nightly warnings to the residents of the danger of fire or of impending air raids, which were certain to come.

As for Helma Graf, she knew she was weaker than a few months before. Whereas she had leaned slightly toward voluptuousness when she and Bill Macneil parted, she was slender now to the point of attenuation. But being lean had no effect on her desire to clasp Bill Macneil to her breasts once again and pull him deep inside her. When not fantasizing about one of her favorite foods like vanilla ice cream (ice was no longer to be had, to say nothing of ice cream), she sank into sleep, lost in reveries about Bill Macneil.

Once she had dreamed about Baron Matsui but had awakened in the midst of the dream to find her face flaming red in the darkness. She chided herself for such a forbidden fantasy and was thankful she had awakened before the dream reached its possible conclusion. She could not allow herself to be unfaithful to Bill even in the darkness of a solitary bedroom.

Will we ever be together? she wondered. Is this ghastly war going on forever and ever? When will men come to their senses and simply say, enough! No more!

A nutritional deficiency had caused blood to ooze from around Helma's fingernails. She wore gloves whenever possible and tried to keep her fingertips wrapped in strips of cloth, but inevitably tiny smears of blood stained the scripts she helped prepare for her two weekly programs at Radio Tokyo.

When Baron Matsui learned the source of the specks of blood on a broadcast script she showed him, he immediately took her to a military clinic in Shinjuku where a doctor of his acquaintance diagnosed the young Swiss woman's condition. He gave her a certificate that allowed her to buy milk and cheese, and the bleeding soon stopped.

On the way back to Radio Tokyo in Kanda, Helma sat beside the baron in the backseat of the sergeant-driven military sedan and allowed him to hold her hand. It would be easy, she thought, to become more intimate with this man, who was perhaps the most appealing Japanese she knew.

"I can't thank you enough, Baron."

"Must you always be so formal, Helma? Surely by now you could call me what my classmates in England always called me—Nobu."

"Perhaps—sometimes when we are alone."

"By the way, I just remembered. When we get to the office, I want to discuss your visiting some POW camps."

"It wouldn't be easy for me to make such trips, would it? Even as a Swiss neutral, I don't think I could go here and there in Japan without—what, an escort or special authorization?"

"We can work that out."

"You want me to talk to some Allied POWs?"

"Exactly, my dear. I could draw up a schedule for you to visit several of the camps and interview maybe a dozen POWs in each one."

"Jeepers, I'd like that."

"Get their names. Find out where they're from. Ask if they have any messages for their families. That sort of thing. I know you have done some of that in your broadcasts already, but I think we should do more."

The plan excited Helma. Tokyo had become a dull and difficult place to live so getting out into the countryside would offer a welcome change.

"But brace yourself, my dear. Conditions in those camps are not, I'm afraid, very good. I'm trying to exert what little influence I have to improve the conditions, but the problem is, how do we feed the POWs enough when our own people are going hungry? Why, do you know only last week they wanted to butcher my horse? Some idiot went to the stable and said horses could no longer be kept for pleasure. Of course, I just laughed at them, but I won't take any chances. I am sending Uranus up to my estate near Ashikaga. He can be put out to pasture there and won't be in any danger when the American B-29s start coming."

Helma shuddered at the prospect of this terrible war being brought so close to home. The baron squeezed her hand.

"By the way, one of the POW camps is up in Ashikaga. There are a number of copper mines there—my family owns several of them—and they've got the POWs mining copper ore. I don't know yet how I will transport Uranus up there, but I'll get him there even if I have to ride him. I thought maybe we could make the trip together, if I take him by train. I could take you to the POW camp and get you inside, then ride Uranus to the other side of the town where we have our property."

Helma turned away. She didn't think she should make a trip like that with the baron. He might take a room next to hers in the local inn or even expect her to stay in his country home. But she did not know how to refuse and still get his approval to make visits to the POW camps. Being able to actually talk in person to American POWs, and send their messages to loved ones at home through their old comrades in the South Pacific, would be good for their morale and for the morale of their families. She felt it was her Christian duty to do this. Just broadcasting to the Allied forces in the South Pacific was meaningless unless she could offer them some cheer and solace and hope that this awful war would soon end and they would be going home. And how overjoyed their families would be to hear from them, even indirectly.

She knew it was her obligation to visit the POW camps and told Baron Matsui that she would.

The first visit, however, was not scheduled for ten days. Meantime, Helma had her broadcasting chores and scavenging for food to sustain the invalid Umeko Macneil, young Shipton—who had become, under her tutelage, an excellent and gratifying performer of the Argentine tango—and the two remaining Macneil servants who were still energetic enough to serve them.

What struck Helma Graf as strange, and in a way perverse about the current state of deprivation in Japan, was that the authorities permitted shortages where there should have been surpluses.

Japan had netted one-third of all the fish caught in the world before the war with more than half coming from adjacent waters.

Yet the people were almost totally deprived of fresh fish, while even dried fish, with its repugnant odor, was never bountiful. And in a country 85 percent of whose surface was heavily forested, charcoal—an absolutely essential item for any housewife's kitchen—was often unavailable.

Add to that the ubiquitous sandals made from rice straw, as plentiful as water and air. Surely, there was no need for straw in the war effort, but the sandals were an item a housewife might spend an entire day looking for to no avail. Helma shook her head in disbelief when she thought about it.

Helma Graf need not have worried about how she might reject his advances when, and if, Baron Nobutaka Matsui tried to enter her boudoir on the trip to Ashikaga. On the day before their scheduled departure, Matsui called her into his office and closed the door.

"I'm sorry, but I can't make the trip to Ashikaga with you, Helma."

Disappointment must have shown in the expressive features of the young Swiss woman, for she assumed her trip was cancelled, too.

"But you're going anyway, my dear," he said, pleasing her greatly. "I've arranged an escort who will register you at an Ashikaga inn and take you to the POW camp. And I've written the orders and requests to permit you to conduct interviews with at least ten of the Americans there."

"Very well, Baron, so if you'll just tell me when I—"

"I'm really sorry about this. I think we might have enjoyed ourselves in Ashikaga." Baron Matsui said this in a way that worried Helma. She had little doubt this man wanted to use this opportunity to become much closer to her, perhaps even to ask her to become his mistress, which was out of the question.

Matsui shook his head in regret. "Were it anything else, I would have refused, but it's quite difficult to say no to the emperor."

"Oh, are you to see His Majesty?" She could not repress her curiosity.

"There's a small group of us army officers who are—what should I say?—quite close to the throne. He likes to have private meetings with us to get our views and opinions. Most of his top advisors, you know, tell him only what the generals and admirals want him to hear."

"I'm sorry you won't be able to go, Baron, but there will be other trips, I'm sure." Helma felt obliged to say that much. Without crossing the line into sexual intimacy, Helma wanted to keep him as an ally. After all, anyone who was close to the emperor. . . .

As she turned to leave, the baron stopped her. "I forgot to mention it, but my horse will be in a boxcar attached to your train. Some fellow from my estate will meet the train at Ashikaga Station, but I wish you would keep an eye on things. You know, make sure Uranus gets off the train safely. Your escort also has been told to be sure Uranus is all right, but I'd like you to make doubly certain."

"Of course."

As she walked out of the baron's office, she almost bumped into Captain Horace Milmay. Helma wondered if he had been trying to eavesdrop.

"I'm leaving for the day, Captain," she told him.

"So early? Who gave you permission?" His pale eyes narrowed in his flushed face.

"The baron. He and I are going on a trip and I must pack a bag."

Helma turned her back on the Englishman and walked away from him, swaying her hips slightly in deliberate provocation. Let him think the baron had become her lover if he liked. It might at least keep Milmay away from her. She wondered if she could do the same thing in reverse to keep the baron at a safe distance.

That night the neighborhood association in the area of the Macneil residence held a firedrill. Helma's attendance was required. She had to wear the shapeless slacks called *mompe* and a padded hood.

A fireman conducted the drill. He hung a smudge pot in a tree. Twenty or so housewives ran back and forth carrying pails of water from a nearby water tank to the tree and heaved the contents of their pails at the fire in the limbs. This was how they would be expected to extinguish fires on rooftops.

At first, few of the women aimed accurately enough to dowse the fire, but after ten or fifteen trips to the tank they began to get the hang of it. By that time, however, the women, who were already weary from their chores of the day, were utterly exhausted, with raw hands and perspiration rolling from under their padded hoods. At last, on unsteady legs they clopped on wooden clogs back to their homes. Helma was so weak she had to rest on the way, even though it was only a short distance to the Macneil residence. At home she packed a small suitcase and tried to get what rest she could before her departure early the following morning.

Her train out of Ueno Station in the north of Tokyo was a *donko* that stopped at every station and sometimes, it seemed, in the middle of rice paddies on its way north. Her escort, a quiet young employee of Radio Tokyo, had something unusual in a Japanese—a pronounced Adam's apple. He had introduced himself to Helma politely enough but seemed to have no interest in carrying on a dialog with her, dozing most of the way.

The rice had been harvested in this northern section of the Great Kanto Plain, with many sheaves still hanging down from the bamboo frames temporarily set up in the paddies. Most of the farmhouses had rows of trees protecting them from the northwest winds out of Siberia, but through the trees Helma caught glimpses of farmers flailing the grain or pushing the sheaves through threshing machines.

As the train approached Ashikaga, her escort roused himself long enough to point out to her the extensive barracks of the POW detention center on the right of the tracks. Then he rose and walked to the forward vestibule.

At that moment it happened.

chapter 19

Ashikaga, Japan
October 1944

Helma Graf had been looking out the train window at the empty POW compound.

Its surrounding high wall, topped with barbed wire, suddenly collapsed, raising a cloud of dust, and partially blocking her view of the one-story frame barracks.

Helma was shocked into silent immobility. Her mind instantly registered earthquake! Her body, however, had not yet reacted. She must have stopped breathing, because she found herself taking a deep gasping breath. The train, decelerating as it pulled into Ashikaga Station, began to rock again, much more than before, from side to side.

She heard a wrenching metallic protest as the couplings on her car twisted away from those cars in front and behind. Shouts arose from passengers. Her car tilted so far to one side, Helma thought frantically, it would turn over completely, but at last it settled back into its normal position, although she could not tell if the wheels were on the tracks or not.

In the town, trees danced about, their branches waving frantically. A fissure cracked open the middle of the street, then closed like a yawning mouth. A few cars and trucks stopped, their drivers climbing down to what they perceived to be safety. One side of the street—a twisted, chaotic tangle—had sunk six feet lower than the opposite side. Dying homes still twisted and squirmed from aftershocks. The frail wooden structures with their light paper-covered *shoji* and crowned with heavy tiles, had splintered into kindling, the tiles sliding down and crashing onto the heaving earth.

One woman was running madly in and out of her shophouse, loading a pushcart with bedding, food, and family treasures. Atop everything sat a canary, its yellow wings beating against its cage. One man lay under a stack of debris, only his waving right arm signaling his existence and location. Others stretched out supine in the street, either dead or too hurt to move.

Helma Graf had heard of the Japanese legend that earthquakes were caused by a giant *namazu*, or catfish, dwelling in mud deep within the earth. This fish was regarded as a rascally fellow, a good-for-nothing with a penchant for practical jokes. He could be restrained only by the Kashima god that guarded Japan from quakes. When this god relaxed his vigilance, the impudent *namazu* thrashed about, wreaking havoc on the countryside.

From her window, Helma could see a young man resembling her escort speeding on foot toward the center of the town. Perhaps he was fleeing for his life, Helma thought. She knew she too should take action of some kind.

Another tremor followed, even more severe than the first.

Passengers in her car began to crawl under the seats, where the spaces were not large enough to accommodate all of them.

Recovering from her momentary shock, Helma felt herself for injury. She found none. Grabbing her overnight kit from the overhead rack, she pushed along the aisle toward the rear of the coach. Men and women were huddled together in the vestibule, as if undecided whether to descend from the train. Helma did not hesitate. She jumped to the ground, looking right, then left. A warehouse by the tracks toward the rear of the train had caved in and was burning fiercely. Several wooden boxcars had overturned near the warehouse, with one dangerously near the flames. Its roof was already smoking.

Helma heard the frantic neighing of a horse. Uranus? It had to be. The baron's horse must be trapped in one of those boxcars. If the overturned boxcar that was already smoking were to catch fire, the flames would spread to the other cars in both directions. Casting aside her overnight kit but with her purse hanging from her left shoulder, Helma began to run toward the neighing horse. Uranus, black with a splash of white on his forehead, was standing nervously in one of the still-upright cars, two cars from the one about to burst into flames. She struggled to unlatch and slide open the door. Helma had never laid eyes on the baron's steed, but she knew this had to be the beloved Uranus. The horse wore a bridle with reins dangling from it. For an Olympic jumper like Uranus, the drop to the ground was no cause for hesitation.

Helma soothed and stroked the animal, then led him to a platform from which she could mount. As a student, she had ridden horses in Pennsylvania but was not an accomplished equestrian by any means. Nonetheless, she gathered her skirt and climbed aboard, using her heels to set the horse in motion. She directed him toward the center of the town, through which, she understood, she would have to ride to reach the Matsui estate on its far side.

She urged Uranus into a canter. The horse, no more eager than she to remain among the fires and pandemonium of the largely destroyed town of Ashikaga, responded with a toss of his well-groomed mane.

Cries of pain and pleas for succor arose from damaged buildings on both sides of the street she rode along. Many of the uninjured stood stunned and silent along the way, evidently undecided about what to do. Some houses had been torn open so their interiors were visible. A few women cradled babies. Others were cramming belongings into cloth bundles. The wall of one woman's bathroom had collapsed, and she stood naked in her wooden bathtub.

In those houses where the housewives had begun their early preparations for dinner by fanning charcoal in the braziers to red coals, these clay pots had overturned, and the women were trying desperately to extinguish smoldering tatami. Many structures, houses and small stores, were fully ablaze. Before one, a young woman was being restrained by two men from plunging back into the doomed house.

Amid the smoke and dust and general bedlam, Uranus cantered northeast. Although many turned from more urgent tasks to stare at Helma, none seemed to register much surprise at seeing a lovely white woman—her supple thighs revealed and her skirt bunched around the waist—riding a black horse through the center of the town. And this a town, it is likely, where no one had seen a white woman in years. White men, yes. The POW compound was there. But not white women. And surely none riding a black horse.

Leaving behind the burning chaos of the destroyed town of Ashikaga, Helma pressed on—frightened and shaken—along a dirt road through rice paddies she hoped would lead her to where Baron Matsui had said his estate lay. Late in the afternoon with an autumn sun beginning to slope toward the west, the air was becoming cooler.

Helma reined in the horse to a slower gait and spoke soothingly. Uranus responded with a snort and a shake of his head. She wondered if the ground still vibrated. It was impossible to tell from the back of a horse in motion.

Ahead, she discerned the back of a man in a civilian suit walking in the same direction she was going. As she drew near, the man turned his face toward her. Pleased, she could see it was her escort from the train. What on earth is he doing here, she wondered.

Helma reined in her horse and spoke in Japanese to the young man, whose name she did not recall. She was puzzled and peevish.

"Why did you run away?"

He still seemed in a state of shock. He mumbled his words and refused to look at her. "I have to hurry to the baron's estate and tell them what has happened. It is my duty."

Helma slid to the ground. "But you left me and the horse behind. Didn't Baron Matsui tell you to look after us? What are you, a coward?"

"If you say so—" He seemed indifferent.

"Anyway, you take the horse and ride on to the baron's place. You know where it is, don't you?"

Numbly, the young man nodded, still too ashamed to look

Helma in the face.

"Tell someone there to let the baron know what has happened."

Helma turned to start walking back toward town, then remembered. "What was the name of the inn where I am to stay?"

"It was destroyed. I just walked past it."

"Well, give me the pass to get into the POW camp."

After some hesitation, the escort handed her an envelope. "It won't do you any good," he said. "The walls around the POW camp were destroyed. Many of the prisoners ran away."

"All of them?"

"Not all. They say there was a full shift down in the copper mines. The mine entrances have collapsed. They are trapped inside."

"But those that ran away: Where did they go?"

The young man from Radio Tokyo shrugged. "Who knows? The guards are out looking for them now. Those damned foreigners are in trouble, you know. The penalty for escape is death."

"But they had to run away," Helma protested. "The earthquake—"

But her escort was not listening. He was leading the horse down the road. Helma wondered why he did not climb on and ride the animal.

Helma was not sure she should reenter the burning town. Dusk was descending. The farmhouses near her were quiet, a few with lights showing. The vibrations from the temblor seemed to have ceased. No farmers were out at their evening chores. Probably, they were huddled inside the flimsy houses, wondering if an aftershock would come in the night. She surmised the last thing they would want at such a time was to offer hospitality to a foreign woman. She would have to seek shelter in a roadside shrine or temple. The nights were cold in October, but not yet unbearable. She would survive, then enter the town tomorrow when it was light and things were calmer.

Suddenly, she realized how famished she was. And how foolish. Why had she opted to return to the town? The fellow from Radio Tokyo knew the way to Baron Matsui's place and was going there. Why had she not gone with him? Why had he not insisted she go? There she would have had a warm bed and a good meal and could have called Tokyo to get instructions from the baron. She knew she had been foolish, but it was too late. She did not know whether it was two miles or five to the baron's estate. To try to find her way along a country road on a dark night would only have compounded her folly.

She had to find a roof before full dark. At least she could get water from one of the clear streams that flowed through this district.

It was not a shrine or a temple where Helma Graf found shelter. It was a modest building that seemed to be a storehouse of sorts with a veranda around three sides. She had learned only about seventy-five of the written characters in Japanese so could not read the entire sign posted in front, but she recognized two of the vertical string of *kanji: kome* for rice and *no* for agricultural, enabling her to surmise this might be a rice storehouse operated by the farmers' agricultural cooperative.

In any case, it was unattended and locked and would provide her with a roof over her head, if she slept on the veranda or in the open space under it. Her slumberous fantasies before dropping off that night did not focus on Bill Macneil or even "Nobu" Matsui but on heaping platters of food. Even dried fish would have been welcome.

Stiff, sore, and famished, she was awakened by sounds in the open field beside the storehouse. She had neglected to wind her watch before going to sleep, but it was full light. It might have been as late as eight o'clock. Coming to her feet, Helma surveyed the immediate vicinity.

The nearest farmhouse was at least a half-mile away. The storehouse was surrounded by rice paddies except for one uncultivated patch of ground—from where came the sounds she had heard. There she saw a squad of Japanese soldiers carrying bayoneted rifles with a booted, sword-carrying officer leading them. They guarded eight—no, nine—Caucasian prisoners. Helma knew they must be Allied POWs from the nearby compound, but she could not determine from their tattered uniforms to what army they had belonged. The prisoners wore hoods over their heads and had their hands bound behind their backs. They stood in a line at a distance of nearly 50 yards from Helma. She took care to keep out of sight behind a corner of the rice storehouse.

The Japanese officer shouted unintelligible orders. In compliance, three of his soldiers began to remove the hoods and bonds from the POWs.

The officer shouted, "*Ki wo tsuke*," and the prisoners wearily came to an indifferent posture of attention.

They were given shovels or other digging tools, probably taken from neighboring farmhouses. At the officer's order, they slowly and reluctantly started to dig a pit. The soldiers aimed their bayoneted rifles at the digging crew. The officer squatted down and began to write on a paper he had smoothed out on his right knee.

Pangs of hunger gnawed at Helma Graf's stomach. She wondered if the opportunity to steal one of the *hango* attached to each soldier's waist would present itself later. She prayed that it would. The rice and pickled vegetables would be welcomed. She also considered sneaking away on the other side of the storehouse and striking out for town, but something stopped her.

When at length a pit had been dug, the prisoners were allowed to rest for a few minutes, then called to a lax attention once more. The officer began to read to them what he had written. At that distance, Helma could not distinguish his words, but they must have been in English, for the POWs seemed to understand. They began to move about and shout. Only the bayonets leveled at their chests held them in place.

When he had finished, the Japanese officer walked to within a couple of feet of the POWs and waved the paper in their faces.

Before each of the nine POWs, he paused for an instant to thrust the paper in the man's face as if asking if he understood it. Obviously excited, he was shouting at the prisoners, and they were saying something back to him. Finally, he came to the last of the nine POWs—a large strapping fellow—who snatched the paper from the hand of the officer. Then he turned, unbuckled his belt, dropped his trousers, and bent over with his buttocks exposed to the officer.

Slowly and deliberately, he wiped his anus with the paper, turned back around, and flung it in the face of the officer, who was jumping up and down and screaming in rage. The offending POW raised his middle finger at the officer, but the other eight prisoners were less demonstrative and remained slumped over and seemingly resigned.

The officer drew his sword and had his soldiers align the POWs along the side of the open pit. They made these Allied soldiers kneel, facing the pit. Helma gasped.

The soldiers forced the POWs to lean forward so their necks were exposed and their heads were above the edge of the pit. The officer uncapped his canteen and poured water down the bared blade of his sword, which glittered in the morning sun.

Taking a stance behind the first POW, the officer shouted and lopped off the man's head. Two soldiers behind the headless trunk used their feet to shove it into the pit.

The officer took two paces down the POW line and repeated the performance. He was obviously a swordsman of considerable skill. Only when he came to the fifth POW did he encounter some difficulty. Three slashes were necessary to completely sever the head. After that the officer carefully examined his blade and poured more water down its length. He dispatched the remaining four prisoners with a single stroke each. After directing his squad to fill in the grave, the officer fell to cleaning his sword, as if any nicks found on the blade would be of greater consequence than the deaths of nine human beings.

Helma Graf was stunned. She clung to consciousness only with difficulty. Her emotions ran from rage to sheer terror and back again. Never, never had she imagined she might witness such an atrocity, and at such close range. Worse, never had she dreamed the Japanese, to whose spiritual welfare she had determined to devote her missionary career, could so callously kill men who were defenseless. She was horrified to the point of nausea. She almost retched right there in her hiding place.

Were these the people whom she had defended so vehemently in her debates with Bill Macneil? Could these cruel, insensate barbarians be the ones she had argued were decent human beings like all others on the planet? Had she and her parents wasted their years of effort on behalf of these animals? No, she took that back.

Even animals could not be as savage and brutal as these caricatures of human beings. Calling them animals was to praise them.
Using words that had never before sullied her lips, in her mind
she called them "*fucking, bloody bastards.*"

Let the B-29s come, Helma prayed to her God with closed
eyes. Let them come in great swarms and bomb this heathen
country to shreds and tatters. Let all the men be emasculated. Let
all these people live out their years in miserable serfdom. More
power to the American forces! Let Bill Macneil and his comrades
fire their machine guns until the barrels glowed red. Let the badg-
ers and Karafuto ravens gorge on mountains of unburied Jap
dead.

In a few hideously cruel moments Helma Graf had been converted from a devotee of peace, a lover of all mankind, into a
vengeful, bloodthirsty advocate of war and slaughter and gory
cruelty in battle.

In college she had been forced to read the then repellent
poems of Rudyard Kipling, but now lines from those verses came
back with a fresh charm and new appeal:

> They will feed their horse on the standing
> crop, their men on the garnered grain;
>
> The Thatch of the byres will serve their fires
> when all the cattle are slain.

Falling to her knees, Helma sobbed quietly for five minutes
or so, then staggered away from the storehouse, keeping it
between her and the squad of soldiers, across the rice paddies
toward Ashikaga. Her hunger was forgotten, replaced by a vora-
cious appetite for vengeance. How could she continue with her

life? How could she keep on in her job? How could she escape from this dreadful country? Why couldn't women don uniforms? Why couldn't she seize a weapon and take up her position beside her lover in battle and charge, screaming at these hateful monsters?

It was almost midmorning when Helma reached Ashikaga. Tears still streamed from her eyes. Coming toward her on the road from town came a wondrous—and welcome—sight: a gold Packard. It was approaching fast, churning dust behind it. Climbing out of a paddy, Helma stumbled into the middle of the road and raised her arms in a plea for the car to stop. It did. Baron Nobutaka Matsui ran toward her.

"Thank God, I've found you!"

Helma lowered her arms and stood disconsolate before him.

He took her hands. "Are you all right, Helma?"

Numbly, she nodded.

"I've driven all night. When I heard about the earthquake, I bribed a supply sergeant to issue me some gasoline, and I started right away. It took longer than I expected since so many roads were impassable." He led the Swiss woman to the waiting car.

"Your horse is all right," Helma told him numbly. "He should be on your estate now."

Helma noticed a suspicion of moisture in the baron's eyes. She wondered if they were tears of gratitude inspired by her safety—or that of his beloved Uranus—or both.

CHAPTER 20

Tokyo, Japan
October 1944

Ill blows the wind that profits no one.

The same might be said of earthquakes, although it is certain Dr. Chinda Nishikawa of the Rikken Laboratory would not have thought of it that way.

Early in October, Doctor Nishikawa had been summoned to Imperial General Headquarters in Tokyo. He was escorted to a third-floor office where two admirals and two generals waited. All wore grim yet expectant expressions. One was the Prime Minister; the second, the Chief of the Naval General Staff; the third, the Chief of the Army General Staff; and the fourth, the recently appointed head of the Army Air Force. In fact, the fourth was Lt.-Gen. Kenji Doihara, who had been transferred from Shanghai in late September.

The questions asked and the replies given at this ultrasecret conference were dutifully recorded by a secretary who was an army captain.

This captain later summarized the conference and had each participant initial the original of the summary, which read:

"In response to questions, Dr. Chinda Nishikawa of the Rikken Laboratory stated one atomic bomb had been manufactured and was ready for testing. If this test is successful, four or five or perhaps even six more such weapons could be made ready in three months. If not successful, then the next test would be made in February, and the completed weapons might be delivered to the armed forces in late summer or fall of 1945.

When asked about arrangements for testing the bomb now ready, Dr. Nishikawa proposed it be placed on an uninhabited island in the Nampo Archipelago directly south of Tokyo, to be detonated by remote control. The bomb would be transported from the Tokorozawa Ordnance Depot to the port of Yokohama. The doctor expects the navy to provide a small ship of shallow draft in order to land the bomb on the island, which has no bays or unloading wharfs.

Assuming that this test—or certainly the second one—will be successful, the participants

in the conference proceeded to a discussion
of how best to utilize the six or so atom
bombs with which the Rikken Laboratory
will equip our armed forces. There followed
a spirited discussion about whether the bombs
should be used on land or at sea, against fleets
of ships or armies. At 11:29 a.m., no consensus
having been reached, the prime minister ended
the meeting saying the situation would have to
be reviewed when the date of the availability
of the bombs became definite.

The navy chief averred the transport vessel
would be ready for loading three days hence,
but wanted the bomb delivered to the navy
port of Yokosuka, not Yokohama. Dr. Nishikawa
stated the bomb would arrive in Yokosuka the
day before. He said he wanted to accompany
the bomb to the testing site but the prime
minister would not approve his application."

Nishikawa watched the 400-ton navy supply vessel Juhachi-go leave its dock in Yokosuka. There was a prayer in his heart as he turned to look for his driver for the trip back to Tokyo.

At the same time, Helma Graf was aboard a train headed for Ashikaga. Just as her train was pulling into the station at Ashikaga and Nishikawa's automobile was nearing the Rikken Laboratory; the earthquake struck at a Richter scale impact of 7.1, nearly as powerful as the temblor that laid waste to Yokohama in September 1923.

The earthquake spawned a tsunami, or tidal wave, that caught up with the atom bomb-laden navy supply ship before it reached the midway point in its voyage to the Nampo Archipelago. The ship did not have time to turn its prow into the monstrous wave, so the 36-foot-high tsunami took the smallish vessel full on its port side and flipped it over. One moment the vessel was steaming full ahead at 18 knots, the next, it was on its side and sinking fast. Nothing floated free of the ship to suggest where it had foundered.

Japan's first completed atom bomb sank into what is known among oceanographers as the Japan Trench, whose bottom is at 27,599 feet.

CHAPTER 21

Shanghai, China
November 1944

The American B-29s had begun to prepare for the fire bombing of Tokyo.

In Europe, after landing in Normandy on D day, the Allied armies had blasted through the hedgerows of northern France and across Belgium and were closing on the German border. From the east, swarms of revenge-thirsty Russians pressed their Nazi foes. Despite the Allied onslaughts and day and night bombing, German war production was increasing and Hitler had a trick or two left up his sleeve.

In Shanghai, Sarah Macneil found herself snagged neatly on the horns of a nasty dilemma.

In September, General Doihara had been called to Tokyo to head the Army Air Force. While no flier, he had a large talent for administration. Before he left, the general took Sarah aside and made it clear he was smitten with her, which she knew full well, and that Tokyo would be a sad and lonely place without her viva-cious presence. Would she come? Sarah demurred. When the gen-eral pressed his suit, insisting she was the most beautiful and desirable woman of his acquaintance, with becoming hesitation Sarah asked for time to consider. Doihara agreed to wait—but only for a brief period.

If Sarah agreed to an "arrangement" with him, she would move far up the ladder and become an intimate of a ranking lumi-nary in the Supreme Imperial Headquarters. With the ear of Kenji Doihara to whisper into on most nights, it was logical she could influence the treatment of her Jews in Shanghai.

The pressing question was, would she have risen too high? What if no mention was ever made of those Jews in Imperial councils? Even in Shanghai, Doihara had never been keenly inter-ested in the Jews in Pootung or the other segregation centers. In Tokyo, his interest might well dwindle to zero.

If Sarah stayed in Shanghai as the occasional sleep-in play-mate of Colonel Kazuo Ishihara, however, the Jews would remain her daily concern. She could visit Pootung daily. She could employ her considerable wiles, when needed, to push Ishihara in one direction or another, or to improve Pootung conditions, or even to prevent or ameliorate a possible calamity.

But such tactics were strictly a local concern. Strategy came from Tokyo, and it was strategy that should have concerned Sarah Macneil.

Shortly before, Tokyo had announced a magnificent naval victory over the Americans off Formosa. Many American war-ships—including "all their carriers"—had been sunk, it was reported. Although the victory was a grotesque exercise in self-delusion, the emperor had declared a national holiday—the first since the disaster perpetrated on the U.S. Pacific fleet at Pearl Harbor.

Sarah pretended she was as pleased as everyone else on the colonel's staff. She dressed in brighter colors than usual and applied with care what little makeup she used. (Mrs. Chang cautioned Sarah that her eyes and lips had too much natural appeal to require much in the way of artificial enhancement.) She asked the amah to warm the rice wine and bring in sushi from a Japanese provisions shop down the street, then gave her the rest of the day off.

Upon arrival the Japanese officer seemed more interested in the hospitality Sarah could provide in her bedroom. Once that hunger was appeased, he donned a robe against the early chill and repaired to Sarah's neat living room to sample the sake and vinegared rice.

"What a glorious victory," Sarah said after pouring his second cup.

Tossing back the wine, the colonel raised a quizzical eyebrow at Sarah.

"You know, Hsiao-mai," Ishihara said, using the Chinese name he preferred to call her these days, "there's a word in English I'm trying to recall. What was it? Ma . . . malar . . . something or other."

"Malarkey?"

"That's it! Malarkey. It means something like nonsense, doesn't it?"

Sarah nodded.

"Do you believe we actually sank almost the entire American fleet off Formosa?"

Sarah had not believed the story, but she had to be careful.

"Well, it does seem a trifle—what should I say, exaggerated?"

"You're right. There's almost no truth to the report. I think the government is doing more harm than good in making such preposterous claims."

In silence, Sarah refilled her lover's *sakazuki*.

"Anyway, we got a national holiday out of the falsehood, so let's enjoy ourselves." He reached for a piece of rice wrapped in seaweed, then dipped it in soy sauce.

"By the way," Ishihara said, taking a bite of sushi, "Colonel Kahner has been making trouble again." He wiped his fingers on a damp cloth, then lit a Golden Bat cigarette.

"He has?"

"Yes. He wants to segregate and isolate our German Jews on an island in the mouth of the Yangtze."

Alarm shivered through Sarah. To disguise the shock she could not conceal, she stood and went to the window. Taking a few breaths to collect herself, she asked, "To what purpose?"

Ishihara puffed on his cigarette and shrugged his shoulders. "The same old story, I suppose. If he gets the German Jews out on that island, he can begin his Final Solution without our interference. He can dispose of them at his convenience and dump their bodies in the ocean. Large schools of sharks congregate in those waters to feed off the garbage thrown overboard before the ships dock in Shanghai."

Dear God, a panicked Sarah gasped to herself, this is just what I've feared. Three thousand of my people. Nathan Blum would be shivering in his Manchurian grave. She could hardly breathe.

"Can Colonel Kahner do this?"

Ishihara inched forward on the sofa, displaying a worried

frown. "Conditions have changed, Hsiao-mai. For one thing, General Kotsuji hates the Jews, although I'm not sure why."

Sarah knew Jiro Kotsuji had replaced Kenji Doihara as commandant of Japanese forces in the Shanghai region. She had not met him face to face but sensed Ishihara did not like him.

"How did this come about?" She struggled to keep her voice steady.

"The story I heard is that Germany supplied us with a shipment of some vital ore in return for our agreement to give the Gestapo a free hand in dealing with the 3,000 German Jews in Pootung. The order to cooperate with Colonel Kahner came directly from Imperial General Headquarters in Tokyo to General Kotsuji."

"Couldn't General Doihara do anything?" Hsiao-mai was itching with anxiety. She wanted to leap up and fly out the door to Pootung, to warn them to flee. If only she had found the means sooner to arm her Jews.

"Doihara's only concern right now is the Army Air Force."

"Couldn't you send me to Tokyo and let me plead with him to help?"

Suspicion distorted Ishihara's features. Hsiao-mai realized she had made a tactical blunder. Ishihara would never allow her to travel to Tokyo, especially to see the man he knew was trying to steal her away from him. So, hastily she added, "Or perhaps you could go."

The colonel relaxed and sank back in the sofa. "I'd have to have some pretext for such a trip and I can't think of one. Later maybe. Besides, we have some time. Kahner has found his island, but facilities have to be constructed. That can't be done overnight. Let's think about it."

And think about it Sarah Macneil did. Long and hard. Through the succeeding days and weeks.

One day she would conceive a certain solution, the next day another. Ideas raced through her mind, some arousing perfervid enthusiasm, only to be dashed by disappointing reality.

Her first inspiration was to hire a Chinese hatchet man to assassinate Col. Gerhardt Kahner of the Gestapo. That would slow them down, she reasoned, but it would only postpone the inevitable. After all, Kahner was hardly the progenitor of the Final Solution. If he died, someone else would take his place to follow the same orders.

Sarah recalled the FEZ project of the Blums. Could it possibly be resurrected? Not in Manchuria, of course, but maybe in Formosa? That was close to Shanghai and needed industrial development. Three thousand skilled, industrious workers could do wonders for Japanese factories producing munitions and supplies there for Japan's armed forces. She spent three days writing up her proposal, handing it to Kazuo Ishihara when next he visited her apartment. He laughed after he read it.

"You really are devoted to these Jews, aren't you?"

"You have sympathy for them, too, don't you?"

"I do. A lot. In fact, I rather like them. But I would have to submit your proposal through General Kotsuji, and I'm sure he would only throw it in the trash."

"Maybe if you sent it directly . . . to Tokyo."

"Without going through channels?" He smiled. "I'd be shipped straight to combat in the Philippines or Saipan or some hellish place. No, I'm too comfortable here in Shanghai—with you."

Sarah's next plan was to try one of her earlier schemes.

Somehow she would arm her Jews and get them on to boats going up the Yangtze. Eventually, they would enter Chinese Communist territory, and the Reds would do anything, she hoped, to thwart the Japanese and the Germans. But how to arm 16,000—or even 3,000—people? How to get enough river boats to transport them up the Yangtze?

By the end of November, she was no closer to a practical way of realizing their salvation. Then came the news the Americans had begun fire bombing Tokyo.

Obviously, momentous changes were coming soon.

CHAPTER 22

Morotai, Moluccas and
Negros, Philippines
November 1944

The final winter of the war.

On the 20th of October, Allied forces under MacArthur landed on Leyte in the Philippines. Although a successful invasion in force, it was only a toehold on an archipelago of 7,100 islands, great and small. A top priority of MacArthur's intelligence staff was learning where on those heavily wooded islands the Japanese were dug in—in what strength, how well they were equipped and supplied, when reinforcements and replacements were scheduled, what were their unit designations, and who were the top generals?

In Europe, the Germans were fighting a desperate and ferocious war on two fronts. Three, really, with Allied armies pushing up the boot of Italy. The German general staff had to assign priorities. Campaigns of lesser importance would have to be scaled down—or abandoned. The extermination of "Europe's undesirables" in near-at-hand death camps might continue unabated, but the minor decimations, such as proposed for the 3,000 German Jews in Shanghai, could no longer be pursued with the previous vigor. Col. Gerhardt Kahner of Shanghai was recalled to the Fatherland to contribute his considerable talents to the administration of local abattoirs. The submarine carrying the good colonel was sunk en route in the Indian Ocean, a British destroyer opening fire while it was surfaced to recharge its batteries.

The loss of German interest in the welfare of the Pootung Jews was noted in Shanghai, gratefully by many, at about the same time as the Japanese government in Tokyo lost interest in fulfilling its obligations under the Axis Tripartite Treaty. With that danger past, Sarah Macneil was ready to give more serious consideration to the ardent invitation she had received to live in Tokyo.

Realizing the Allied net was closing, Japan constructed a plan to win the war in the Philippines before MacArthur and Nimitz could push any closer. The plan formulated six routes to victory, utilizing all the Imperial forces in the Philippines as well as those that could be dispatched there in short order. The order of battle—that most precious of military secrets—was laid out in startling detail. Precise numbers and locations of all Japanese units in the Philippines were listed.

If the Americans could only clap their avid eyes on this plan, it would be an intelligence coup equal to breaking the MAGIC and ENIGMA codes earlier in the war. That acquisition of the plan, Operation Z, might just be possible, was a fantasy on the order of the sinking into the deep Japan Trench of the five main Japanese islands.

Yet, that vague possibility actually began to materialize when Adm. Shigeru Fukudome boarded a four-engine Kawanishi "Emily" flying boat that left Davao on Mindanao, headed on a dog-leg route northeastward toward Cebu.

Admiral Fukudome carried a waterproof dispatch case containing a red-covered copy of the crucial Z Plan; its name was taken from the Z on the flag hoisted by Admiral Heihachiro Togo before the glorious Battle of Tsushima Straits forty years earlier.

In the channel between Cebu and Negros, the Emily ran into a violent tropical storm, crashing in shallow water off Negros. As it began to burn, the radioman reported to Japanese headquarters in Manila the crash location. He requested immediate assistance for the injured admiral, himself, and the three surviving crewmen. As the large seaplane began to settle, the survivors loaded the semiconscious Admiral Fukudome, still clutching his dispatch case, into a rubber raft and rowed to the nearby beach. Miserable and unarmed, the airmen awaited the requested help from Manila.

Sighting the flames, a band of Filipino guerrillas reached the survivors before Japanese rescuers could arrive. They shot the four Japanese crewmen. One of the guerrillas had spent a year in Japan before the war and had a slight acquaintance with things Japanese. He realized that Fukudome, unconscious from loss of blood, was a high-ranking naval officer. The guerrilla stayed the hands of the Japanese officer's would-be executioners.

The wife and two children of a guerrilla leader had been taken hostage by the local Japanese unit, whose colonel was making various demands on the Negros guerrillas in exchange for the three hostages. Now, these guerrillas calculated, with such an important Japanese officer in their grasp, they could counter the demands of the Japanese colonel. Accordingly, they improvised a stretcher and carried Admiral Fukudome through the jungle to their camp. The following morning, the guerrilla who had lived in Japan examined the admiral's belongings and found the red-covered Z Plan. Under the title he saw the two ideographs that read *Gokuhi*—meaning Top Secret. The guerrilla recognized only the second ideograph—'*hi*'—and its meaning of secret.

With his radio transmitter, the guerrilla leader quickly sent a message to their usual contact in MacArthur's intelligence division in Australia:

> HAVE CAPTURED HIGH-RANKING JAP
> OFFICER SERIOUSLY INJURED AND
> UNCONSCIOUS. DISPATCH CASE HOLDS
> 32-PAGE SECRET DOCUMENT. REQUEST
> YOU SEND TRANSLATOR TO EXAMINE
> DOCUMENT. WE WILL REPLACE
> DOCUMENT IN DISPATCH CASE AND
> RELEASE ADMIRAL IN EXCHANGE
> FOR OUR HOSTAGES HELD BY LOCAL
> JAPANESE. THEY MAY NOT LEARN
> DOCUMENT HAS BEEN COMPROMISED.

The Americans had landed a large invasion force on Morotai in the Moluccas on September 15, 1944. The 32nd Division with its long combat record was still mopping up. Attached to the 32nd was an ATIS team commanded by Capt. Bill Macneil. It was to him that a top-priority message from Indooroopilly in Australia was addressed, followed within hours by another black C-47 to fly Bill and one assistant to Negros in the southern Philippines.

MacArthur was already on Leyte, and his next move would be to land on Mindoro December 15th. Mindoro lay beyond Cebu, Negros, and Panay, so the chief of staff in Washington regarded this plan as highly dangerous, because it would leave the Allied invasion fleet open to flank attacks from the many Japanese bases on the other islands along the route to Mindoro. MacArthur, who considered himself superior in both strategic and tactical conceptualization to the Washington brass—including George Marshall and Ernest King—ignored their advice.

However, he did recognize the danger on his flanks and deemed it essential that he know exactly where these enemy bases were located. Therefore, he literally *jumped* for joy—according to one of his incredulous aides—when Courtney Whitney, the former Manila lawyer who was intelligence chief for the Philippine campaign, informed him of the capture of certain secret documents.

Immediately, MacArthur summoned Col. Sidney F. Mashbir, commanding officer of ATIS, giving him precise orders emphasizing that heads would be separated from torsos if "The Boss" was not fully satisfied with the results of the ATIS mission to Negros.

After landing by parachute on Negros, Bill Macneil and Slats Honda were led by a guerrilla welcoming party to their camp under the trees some three miles from the coast where the two ATIS men would be met by a submarine the following day for their return trip.

Sergeant Honda was still grumbling. "How many more times we gonna have to do this?"

"I thought maybe you had become fond of parachuting, Slats."

"Me? You gotta be kidding, Captain."

"I told you I could take someone else this time, if you didn't like the altitude."

"I had to come along to protect you, but this is the last time. Next time, you can take one of our gung-ho replacements."

Macneil smiled. He knew Slats Honda would never let anyone take his place on one of their jump missions.

The two translators set to work immediately. Admiral Fukudome had regained consciousness but was still weak and unaware his dispatch case—kept in a separate hut—was being examined. The admiral had been told that the guerrillas were negotiating with the local Japanese for a hostage exchange. He had been given such medical treatment as the guerrillas were capable of, and would likely survive.

After studying what they learned at once was called the Z Plan, Macneil told Honda, "These people were right. This is incredible stuff. It's the entire Japanese order of battle for the Philippines. Here, see for yourself. . . ."

Macneil decided a translation would take too long, so he had Slats make a photocopy with the tiny Minox 16mm camera he carried. Bill also decided against trying to interrogate the injured admiral, which might only arouse his suspicions that his dispatch case had been opened and the Z Plan compromised. They avoided the admiral's hut and would leave the next morning for their evening rendezvous with the American submarine.

That night they were given bedding in an isolated, seldom-used hut where they were advised to keep an eye open for millipedes and giant centipedes. The former were as thick as a man's thumb and had a bite known to cause blindness. The latter grew to 10 inches and their venom could bring on a high fever and even death.

For breakfast they got rice and carabao meat, served by a dowdy Filipina with whom Slats Honda tried to negotiate a quick sexual interlude. He said, "Push-y, push-y, okay?" But apparently, she knew only Tagalog or was deliberately pretending to be ignorant of Slats's intentions.

It was almost noon when two of the guerrillas started for the coast, leading the two Americans. The distance was only three miles, but they preferred to be cautious, following a longer less-traveled path that led through shoulder-high cogon grass and a tangled jungle of twisted creepers and thorn. Torrential rainfall the night before made the going slippery, and even the jungle-trained guerrillas slid in the slick mud half a dozen times the first two hours.

At length, the guides stopped and said goodbye.

"The trail is better the rest of the way. Just keep going east," the first said, pointing the way.

"You'll be able to see the ocean soon," the second added. "When you come out on the beach, look right and left. You'll see three coconuts piled on the sand. That marks where you should flash your light four times. The submarine should be right off shore. The time was seven-thirty, right?"

Macneil confirmed the rendezvous time, then started down the path with Slats Honda close behind. The Filipinos disappeared into the tall grass.

When two hours had passed, Macneil and Honda rested and ate their last K-rations. As they were tossing the debris of their meal deeper into the jungle, a Japanese patrol appeared walking single file up the trail toward them. Both parties saw each other at the same instant.

The Japanese were armed with Arisaka .25-caliber bayoneted rifles. Macneil carried only his Colt .45, Honda had a .45-caliber grease gun. Because of the narrowness of the trail, only one man could move forward against his enemy at a time.

Macneil had fired his pistol twice and dropped two Japanese by the time the third charged Bill, his bayonet aimed at Bill's midriff.

Firing his grease gun in short bursts, Honda stepped around Macneil to stand in front of him. He killed or wounded three of the enemy, but a fourth charged, yelling in battle lust.

"*Kutabare, kono keto-me!*" ("We've got you, you hairy foreign beasts!")

Striving to get back around in front of Honda, Macneil shouted in reply, "*Kuso kurae, kono chikusho-me!*" ("Eat shit, you bastards!")

Being cursed in their own language must have startled the remaining two Japanese, for they hesitated, then turned as if to flee. But one of the two pulled a grenade from his belt, slamming the fuse against his helmet to activate it. Macneil could see the man's lips moving as he counted. Then he flipped the grenade across the intervening 25 feet separating them.

Macneil's Colt barked a second or two too late, but it was deadly. The grenade-thrower collapsed in a heap; the second darted away through the cogon grass.

The grenade fell to the ground four feet to Macneil's right. He was slow to react, so Honda threw his body on the grenade, which exploded as soon as he covered it.

Or most of it. The explosion blasted a hole in the sergeant's right rib cage. Shrapnel from that part of the grenade not completely covered by the Nisei's body struck Macneil in the upper thigh of his left leg and in the stomach on the right. Bill was knocked off his feet but quickly recovered enough to crawl to his sergeant's side and roll him over to face the sky.

Reloading his Colt, Macneil kept a sharp eye on the path along which the lone surviving Japanese had escaped. He knew the escapee would return soon enough with reinforcements. Bill bandaged Honda's ghastly wound as best he could, but that did not do much to stanch the flow of blood. Honda was only partly conscious.

"Let's rest for a minute, Slats. Then I'll get you to the submarine."

The Nisei laughed weakly. "Don't be a *baka*, Bill. I'm done for. You go on. I'll stay here and hold off those fucking gooks when they come back."

"You think I'd leave you here? Just take a few more breaths and we're on our way."

"You dumb bastard, man. I'm dying. You got the film, right? Get your ass outta here." Honda's voice weakened, and he coughed. "And listen, when the war's over, give my love to that Little Orphan Annie of yours."

Holstering his pistol, Macneil lifted the sergeant to his feet and hoisted him onto his right shoulder. He began to stagger down the trail toward the coast. He could feel his own blood flowing down his left leg and right side and knew he had to hurry to reach the rendezvous before he fainted himself.

For the first eight or ten minutes, he heard Honda groan occasionally. When the groans stopped, he lowered the Nisei to the ground.

His best friend was dead. Bitter tears blurred Macneil's vision. There was no time to bury Slats, so Macneil dragged the body into the jungle. He cut the two dog tags from their neck-thong and pushed one into Honda's mouth. The other he pocketed. There was no other identification on his friend's body. Only a clasp knife and a gold tooth. Macneil wondered if Honda had taken the tooth from a Japanese body.

A wave of weakness flowed over Macneil when he tried to stand. All that mattered was getting the Z Plan film to MacArthur's intelligence staff. He cut strips from Honda's fatigue shirt and bandaged his own wounds.

If only he could make it to the submarine and then to an air field on Leyte. . . .

chapter 23

U.S. Army Hospital,
Australia
April 1945

Capt. Bill Macneil had been in the hospital in Indooroopilly for four and a half months.

On December 15, MacArthur's forces landed on southern Mindoro right on schedule. Manila fell on February 5th. The Philippines campaign was hard fought, but victory was assured the U.S by knowledge of the Z Plan—without Japan's ever realizing it had been read by enemy eyes.

President Franklin Roosevelt died on April 12; Harry Truman of Missouri had taken the oath to serve in his place.

The heaviest fire bombings of Tokyo occurred on March 10 and April 6, even though more would follow. Iwo Jima was captured in March.

In Europe, the Germans were on the ropes. It was only a question of time.

The greatest land battle of the war for the Americans was yet to be fought. It would be called *Tennozan* by the Japanese and would be touched off when Allied forces hit the beaches of Okinawa on April 1.

Through these momentous events, Bill Macneil lay in a hospital bed in Australia, fuming with impatience and exasperation. Not that he was such a flame-breathing war lover that he ached to get back into the shooting, but he was grimly anxious to learn about the welfare of Sarah, Shipton, his stepmother Umeko, and—yes, he confessed it freely—Helma Graf.

Stationary for several months, he was gratified when, at last, his mail caught up with him, including a stack of letters yea-high sent via Switzerland and from his father's address in Oregon.

The two shrapnel wounds had not kept Macneil flat on his back so long. Instead, a staphylococcal infection had set in and been devilishly difficult to overcome. The staph germs had proved so stubborn that all infected patients had been isolated in a separate wing of the hospital.

It was to that wing that Col. Sidney Mashbir, head man of ATIS, had come calling one day in February. He was a tall, hearty cigar smoker well liked by subordinates. He wore a thin moustache and parted his hair precisely in the middle.

"Don't sit up, Macneil. Save your strength."

"How are you, sir?"

"I'm fine, but I'm the one to be asking that question."

"I think you have already asked the doctors, haven't you?"

Mashbir nodded, extinguishing his cigar stub under the

severe glare of an army nurse. "I'm here to talk about something else. We've decided to recommend you for the Medal of Honor."

"Commander Rochefort didn't receive the medal for breaking the Japanese navy code, did he?"

"No, the medal has to be won in combat against an enemy, so you qualify. He didn't."

"Anyway, Colonel, I couldn't accept it."

"I have never heard of anyone refusing the Medal of Honor. May I ask you why?"

"Because I don't deserve it as much as my sergeant, Slats Honda. He gave his life to save me. He made it possible for me to escape with the film of the order-of-battle plan. Give it to him, sir, or to his memory. I mean it."

Colonel Mashbir was thoughtful. He stuck an unlit cigar in his mouth. "Well, we will see. I'll talk about it with the staff some more. You take care of yourself." He patted the army nurse on her hip and winked suggestively as he passed.

"I hope you mean that, sir," she said laughing.

"You get our boy here back on his feet and I'll give you a weekend to remember."

"Promises, promises."

Bill Macneil was a different man from the one who had jumped on Negros last November. In appearance, for one thing. He was no longer the gaunt, bones-and-sinew officer of 1944. Hospital fare was good and more than adequate, and the staph germs raging in his wounds did not prevent him from regaining the lost weight. But they weakened him. It was an effort even to sit up in bed, and bedpans were still the rule. His sun-blackened skin had paled, his blond hair kept short and neat from weekly visits by a hospital barber. A nurse shaved him every morning and did a better job than he could have. It was only that damned weakness. On New Guinea he had dreamed of *dolce far niente* vacations, lazy days reading and listening to music, good food brought by attentive, devoted servers, but now, enough was enough.

Nurses from other wards often found excuses to talk to Macneil, apparently attracted to him physically or to his valorous reputation.

Occasionally, ATIS personnel visited, subdued and respectful. They seemed to regard him as one of the gods in their pantheon. The man who brought back the Z Plan, saving thousands, maybe tens of thousands of American lives. Whenever they mentioned it, Macneil invariably reminded them it was Slats Honda they should pay homage to. At least, to his memory.

Until Bill's mail began to arrive, he spent his waking hours reading—he had just finished Kathleen Windsor's best seller *Forever Amber*, there not being much choice in his reading matter—and listening to Radio Tokyo on the radio by his bed. He never missed the programs of Little Orphan Annie. The whole ward fell silent when her voice came over the waves.

Yet, he sensed something had happened to Helma Graf, and he could not understand what it might have been. She still played the same popular and semiclassical music. She still transmitted news about POWs and messages from some of them. But gone were her soft, dulcet tones, replaced by a crispness and a certain— what to call it—a certain glassy, impenetrable quality. She still managed to inject a soupçon of sympathetic commiseration for the POWs into her scripts—perhaps as much as the masters at Radio Tokyo would allow—but somehow or other she was coming across as a different, more mature woman, one not to be trifled with. And she broadcast no more appeals for Allied forces to lay down their arms.

Yes, Macneil was certain Helma had changed, but he had no way of knowing why.

In her letters, too, he discerned this when they began to arrive, usually months late. At first, in letters written early in 1944, she kept up her familiar refrain. "I don't know where thee are, but I pray thee are not engaged in the fighting. Please, oh, please, stay away from all this mad killing. Don't kill thy fellow man and, of course, don't let anyone kill thee. I would die, too, as thee must know."

But in later letters these pleas disappeared. Whatever caused the change in Helma, Bill knew it must have happened suddenly. Nothing gradual about this. It was abrupt and complete. Blackness one minute; bright light the next. Or vice versa.

Gone too was a certain humor and lightness. No more charming asides. No whimsical cautions.

After reading Helma's missives once, he went over all of them again and underlined in pencil those sentences or phrases he wanted to digest and remember. He noted what she wrote about his brother, Shipton: "Ship decided to apply for Japanese citizenship so he could stay with his mother, who is still in bed most of the time. This made him eligible for the draft, but for the present they are leaving him alone because of his asthma." Then later: "The Japanese are scraping the bottom of the barrel for manpower, I suppose, for they have called Ship to duty. He has written he will be trained as a pilot. Can thee imagine little Ship flying one of those deadly Zero fighter planes? I can't."

There was also news about Sarah: "She is in Tokyo. She lives with us, at least most of the time. I think she is very close to Kenji

Doihara. She refers to him as 'Ken-san.' Can thee believe it? Thy little sister calling a lieutenant-general by his first name? He is head of the Army Air Forces now."

In March, Colonel Mashbir came again, accompanied by a staff colonel, a major, and Bill's old friend David Spencer.

Arranging themselves on chairs around the bed, Mashbir cleared his throat. "I'm told you can be up and about pretty soon."

"I feel better, sir. Not quite up to snuff, but better."

"Good. Now, first of all, my congratulations. You're a major. Spencer here brought the orders and a pair of oak leaves."

Macneil nodded his appreciation.

"Also, we've decided to act on your recommendation. We put Sergeant Honda in for a posthumous Medal of Honor, and it was approved."

"Who will accept it on his behalf?"

Mashbir cleared his throat again. "It looks as if you will—if you can get well and fly to Washington."

"Why me, sir?"

The other colonel—a small, dark fellow with infantry rifles on his collar—spoke up. "Well, we tried to talk to his parents. They had been in a relocation center in Idaho, but they left there last year."

Macneil tried to rise up on his elbows in bed. "Left the center? Could they do that?"

"It wasn't compulsory, you know. All they had to do was take the oath of allegiance and they could leave. Anywhere but back to their homes in California. Anyway, they went to Chicago last December, where they were both killed in a car wreck. The next week. We're not sure if they ever learned what—what happened to Sergeant Honda."

Sadly, Macneil shook his head. "Well, Slats must have had other relatives. I heard him mention two brothers."

"And that's all he had. Beside the parents, just the two brothers."

"Well, why can't they accept the Medal?"

"That's the rub, Macneil. They refuse."

"Refuse?"

"That's right." The colonel looked at his hands, clasped on his lap. "It's a sad story. The brothers are pro-Japan. It seems they hate our country. They were born in California and had dual citizenship but refused to take the oath of allegiance. Instead of going to a relocation center with their parents, they were sent to the segregation center at Tule Lake. In California. Except for the war, they would have been shipped to Japan. And they will be, as soon as the war is over. Sergeant Honda, of course, had joined the army before the war, but that really tore the family apart. Brother against brother."

"So that's why Slats hated Japan so much," Macneil mused half to himself.

"What's that?" Mashbir asked.

"He hated the Japanese more than most of the Nisei I've worked with. He always called them 'gooks.' In fact, his last words to me were he could 'hold off the fucking gooks' while I got away."

"Anyway," the colonel said, "the brothers refuse to have anything to do with the Medal of Honor, and you're the only one we can think of to accept the award in his name."

"If that's the case, I'll do it. Of course."

"And you'll be awarded the Distinguished Service Cross at the same time."

Sergeant Slats Honda's award was given to Macneil in the presidential office of the White House. It was late April, and the ATIS major was completely recovered. Once the staphylococcus germs were exterminated, Bill's recovery was almost miraculously swift. In fact, he had recuperative leave coming and planned to use it parachuting in Oregon.

Two other wounded veterans were present at the ceremony, one legless in a wheelchair. Both were given the Medal of Honor by the diminutive man from Missouri who was an artillery captain in World War One.

As everyone was leaving Truman's office, the president asked Macneil to stay behind. The doors were closed, and Macneil found himself alone with Harry Truman.

"Sit down, Major. Tell me, are you completely recovered?"

"I believe I am, sir."

"That's what I wanted to hear, because I have something very important to talk to you about."

Macneil waited quietly.

"I know a lot about you, Major. More than you might think. I've read the dossier on you from military intelligence and we've talked to many other sources. We know all about your family background in Japan. In fact, it might surprise you to learn I had your father fly here from Oregon for a talk." While Truman talked, he strode around his desk. The president was still as stiffly erect as he must have been in the First World War, his eyes enlarged and serious behind his glasses, his accent right out of the Midwest.

"We know your younger half-brother is training to be a Zero pilot, and Sarah Macneil is the part-time mistress of the man who heads the Japanese Army Air Forces."

Macneil grimaced. "So I must suppose, sir, you know my Swiss girlfriend works for Radio Tokyo."

Truman nodded.

Macneil waited for his commander-in-chief to continue. This had to be leading somewhere.

"To tell you that what I am going to talk about is top-secret, son, is obvious. It's so confidential even I—as vice-president—knew nothing about it until after I took the oath of office as president. I'm not going to tell you all I know, but I will say this." Truman returned to his chair. "The United States is developing a truly awesome weapon of war. When it's ready, we may use it against Japan."

"Only against Japan, sir?" Macneil asked.

"I'd rather have used it against the damned Germans first," Truman said, without explaining why, "but they're going to surrender in a matter of weeks. Maybe in days. They'll be out of it and just in the nick of time for them."

Macneil controlled his impatience.

"We'll test our weapon soon," Truman continued. "If the test is successful, we will manufacture a handful of these weapons, and then it will be up to me to decide when—and if—to use them."

"If you don't use these weapons, Mr. President, then what?"

"We land on the beaches of Japan."

"That will mean tens—even hundreds—of thousands of casualties—both American and Japanese, sir." Macneil was appalled at that prospect.

"And if I use this weapon, it will mean just as many. Maybe more."

"Except the casualties would all be Japanese, wouldn't they?"

"Yes, but I didn't call you in to discuss the ethics of my decision. I want to tell you we are certain the Japanese are building a similar weapon. If they have it in time, they're sure to drop it on our men once they have landed on the Japanese beaches."

Macneil kept his peace, a sinking feeling growing within him.

"How would you like to be in Tokyo very soon, Major?"

Macneil's mind leapt ahead. "You want me to somehow slip into Tokyo and try to learn more about Japan's weapon?"

Truman nodded. "Through your sister and maybe your girlfriend."

Dear God, Macneil thought. What am I about to get into?

chapter 24

*From Washington
to Tokyo
June 1945*

Germany surrendered on May 8.

But to Bill Macneil the war in the Pacific was the only war that mattered, and he did not allow the victory festivities in Washington to deter him from preparing to carry out President Truman's mission. Even so, things took longer than Bill had calculated. On one occasion he was forced to call for Harry Truman's intervention—and famous temper—to get things moving.

Macneil's false identification papers caused the delay. In consideration of Switzerland's neutral status and his relationship with Helma Graf, OSS—where military intelligence had gone for assistance—had decided to give Bill Macneil an identity as a Swiss citizen. They rejected fabricating a Swiss passport and instead had tried to find a genuine document. Eventually, they succeeded.

A Swiss named Emil Grimm died of natural causes in Japan in 1940. He was only two years older than Macneil, and Grimm's personal possessions, including his passport and registration certificate for Japan, were bundled up by the Swiss Embassy in Tokyo and shipped to his family in the village of Gandria on the shores of Lake Lugano. By means the OSS saw no need to reveal, the OSS obtained both documents and were able to substitute a recent photograph of Bill Macneil's for Emil Grimm's.

The technical services section of OSS judged these documents adequate for their intended use. To be sure, Herr Grimm had expired in Japan, but his demise was not noted in any of the identity documents. He had died skiing down a dangerous slope in the mountainous prefecture of Aomori. A record of Grimm's accidental death could no doubt be found in the local township near the ski slope or in the Swiss Embassy in Tokyo, but only the most exigent of circumstances would ever persuade a Japanese official to delve so deep. If anyone did pursue the matter that far, the game would be up anyway.

While the documents were being assembled and doctored, Swiss-tailored clothing appropriate to the early summer in Tokyo was made in Bern and shipped through Lisbon and New York to Washington.

The next to last chore on Macneil's Washington agenda was a visit to the submarine command in navy headquarters. That took three days and required another salvo of the president's temper to persuade the underwater sailors to risk one of their precious submersibles in a perilous undertaking.

This undertaking was dangerous enough in other times, but with the entire nation of Japan casting fearful eyes seaward, expecting an imminent American invasion, it approached fool-hardiness.

At length, Truman prevailed and a rendezvous point and two dates (7 and 28 July) were decided upon. On both those dates a U.S. sub would surface briefly, on a moonless night, off the west coast of Izu Peninsula, south of Tokyo. No one expected an invasion there since there were no beaches. Except for a few tiny inlets like Heda and Toi, the mountains dropped steeply into the ocean.

Getting from Tokyo to the west coast of Izu would be left to the ingenuity of Bill Macneil.

The final item on the Washington schedule was to arrange surreptitious entry into Japan. The OSS had dropped hundreds of agents into denied territory in Europe as well as the Near East, but they had no experience in Japan. Indeed, there was no record of any Allied agent ever parachuting into Japan. They would fly Macneil in one of their black aircraft, like those used by ATIS in the South Pacific, from Washington to Honolulu and then to the Marianas, where a final decision about the route would be made.

Macneil's knowledge of the local terrain was more detailed than any of the OSS fliers, who were a wild bunch deeply distrusted by Macneil, so the chutist's expertise would have to be relied on.

Both the pilot and copilot of the camouflaged C-47 complained bitterly most of the way to the drop zone. Their complaints were obviously intended for Macneil's ears. Since he was dressed in the civilian clothing from Bern, they did not know Macneil was a major or even what his name was.

"You must be outta your friggin' mind, buddy, to do this," the pilot snorted over his right shoulder.

"Yeah, how much they paying you?" the copilot asked.

"Why? You want to go in my place?"

"You crazy? We've dropped a lot of assorted types into France but never anyone out here."

"Jesus, Smitty, would you look at that!" the copilot's voice rose.

Far ahead of them, in the darkness, they could see what looked like a sea of fire. The *Edo no hana*—the fires of Tokyo—were blooming again. As the C-47 neared the city from the north, tracers from antiaircraft batteries could be observed climbing erratically toward the heavens.

"Jesus, we're not flying into that, are we?" the copilot asked, fingering a rosary.

"I'll get off just west of all that commotion," Macneil told the men in the cockpit. "Then you fellows can go back the way you came."

"I know, I know," the pilot said. "I'm just glad all those Superforts will be winging it south after their bomb runs."

"They were warned to watch out for one lonely little Gooney Bird."

"Yeah, yeah, but there're more than three hundred of those bastards. Do you think all of them will remember? They don't give one shit about us. All they're thinking about is dropping their incendiaries and hauling ass. Back to Saipan to sack out for a couple of days."

"While we gotta deadhead all the way back to ole D.C.," the copilot moaned.

"I bet you'll have yourselves a nice layover at Hickham. Anyway, it's been nice talking to you fellows, but I've got to get ready."

"Will you recognize some landmarks?"

"There's a dam right close to Mount Takao. Just don't dump me in that lake behind it."

"You know the place?"

"I used to swim there when I was a boy, but I don't feel like a dip right now, thank you."

The jump onto the low mountain was easy. Macneil came down among trees near the Yakuoin Temple of the Shingon sect. It was a dark night, the chute was black, and his Swiss-made suit was dark blue. The temple was built in the 700s and was too small to have a resident priest. Untangling himself, Macneil shoved the parachute under some undergrowth off the trail leading past the temple, down the 1,800-foot hill of Takao.

A short way down the deserted trail, he passed *Biwa-taki,* or Lute Falls, where he and Sarah had cavorted as youngsters. Nothing seemed changed in the eight or nine years since their visit.

Toward the east, Tokyo's conflagration seemed to be leaping higher than ever into the night sky. The last wave of B-29s had flown west, directly toward Mount Takao, but had veered south to begin their wide sweep toward the Pacific.

It would be a long tiring road to his family home in Tokyo, if the house still stood after the holocaust, but he could not imagine a better time to make the trek. There would be little room in the minds of any of the largely reduced population of Tokyo, or its western environs, to heed anything but the blazing emergency around them. Even in broad daylight, Macneil would not be instantly recognizable as a Caucasian foreigner, with his low-brimmed hat and the gauze face-mask most Japanese wore over their noses and mouths during air-raids, to avoid breathing embers and hot ash. In any case, in the worst scenario, he carried identification as Emil Grimm, a citizen of a neutral nation.

If Macneil had to walk all the way home, he might not be able to complete the trip in one night, but he hoped to find a stray bus running toward the city. He knew the electric cars on the Chuo line would not be moving during an air raid of this magnitude, but they might start up after the all-clear. That would depend on how much debris was on the tracks and how quickly it could be cleared. If he could board a Chuo train at one of the intermediate stations, he could ride it into Shinjuku station and transfer to a line that would pass within a mile or so of the Macneil home in Azabu. If not, it would be a long, long walk— and one he vastly preferred to make in the dark.

As he trudged farther down the hill, Bill thought about what he had heard had happened to his hometown in recent months. Since November, B-29s from their bases in the Marianas, supplemented by planes from the carrier task force of Admiral Halsey's Third Fleet parked off-shore, had pummeled Japan's capital in an endless series of strikes. The most damaging was on the night of 9-10 March.

On that fateful evening, 300 Superfortresses had unloaded 700,000 bombs on a 3-by-4-mile square of central Tokyo. The bombs were the new M29s carrying the evil mixture of incendiary jelly and oil called napalm.

That bomb load was ten times the weight of all the bombs dropped by the German Air Force on London during all the great fire raids in September 1940. The area razed in Tokyo was fifteen times the surface laid waste in the capital of England four and a half years before.

Macneil was able to board the final train of the night at Koganei station after a two-hour hike over dark, deserted roads. He bought a ticket with the Japanese yen he had been given in

Washington and boarded the last coach of the seven-car train. It was very crowded, which enabled him to huddle in a corner with his face pressed against a window.

All the passengers appeared to be about to drown in their own misery. Some were injured, with bloody makeshift bandages around hands or necks. Most were sprinkled with ash, burnt holes visible here and there in their clothing. The shapeless *mompe* was the universal garb for women. The men wore puttees and padded jackets, some with hoods. Almost all had gauze masks over their mouths and noses. About half carried bundles or knapsacks. No conversation was audible over the rattle of the rocking train, only coughs and clearing of throats and an occasional gasp or low moan. No one looked at Macneil in his corner at the end of the coach. He wondered where the children were. He saw none.

He transferred at Shinjuku station on the west side of Tokyo, but still had not seen any razed districts, although evidence of the fire storm still churning the air over the center of the capital was plentiful. On the station platform, he passed a weary-looking policeman who eyed him suspiciously but who must have decided this was no time to be interrogating passersby, however odd they might appear.

It was past three in the morning when Macneil began walking down the familiar but empty street that led from Arisugawa Park past Gama Pond, famous as the site of a grisly murder in bygone days, toward the old Matsukata mansion on a cliff overlooking the Juban district. No lights were showing, probably because the B-29 raid had interrupted electric service. No matter. He and Shipton had known every hidden alleyway, every obscure path, every back entrance in this neighborhood. He walked cautiously and quietly around to the rear of the Macneil compound, wondering who would be in his home. According to Helma's last letter, only one of the former family retainers was still living there, and she had not thought he would be with them long. Shipton was in uniform, and hadn't his stepmother been sent to Nagasaki for safety? That might leave only Helma and Sarah in residence.

Macneil remembered he could dislodge a brick from the high wall in back for a toehold. From there to the tree he could shinny up and step over to the roof leading to a window of his room. On the top limb he paused to catch his breath and look around. One wing of the large home was gone, doubtless burned in an earlier raid.

Macneil was filled with a sudden sweet melancholy. This was the place of his birth. The home where he and Shipton and Sarah had grown up. Ah, the days of his youth. It was a regret he could not articulate. So long ago, but really not that many in years. He had gone to California only four years before, happy to leave Japan—but not this old house with so many pleasant memories.

The house was dark, as he had expected. He wanted to get inside, out of the ash-filled air, which even here carried a charred smell. Off to the east, the fires that had consumed the city he had known so well had begun to diminish.

The window to his bedroom opened easily. Tokyoites did not take precautions against burglars, at least not during this season of travail.

Quietly, he entered his old room, where Helma had written she now slept. Dimly, he could see his bed was where it had been in August 1941. God, he had been only twenty-two then. Now, nearly four years later, he felt well into middle age.

Cautiously, he stole past his bed, intending to go into the hall and down the stairs, but he heard someone roll over, then saw a dim shape sit up in the semidarkness.

chapter 25

Tokyo, Japan
June 1945

The light switch was where Macneil remembered.

He flipped it on, but the room remained dark. He had forgotten the electric stoppage.

"Dare desu ka?" There was a quaver in the voice from his bed, asking who was there.

"It's me," he answered. "Bill."

"Bill? My God, what are you doing—"

He sat on the edge of the bed. His eyes had adjusted enough for him to discern—dimly—that his bed's occupant was a female—a naked one.

"Cover yourself, you shameless wench." He tried to insert a light tone into his voice.

"Why should I? You've seen me naked often enough," the woman said, moving to his side and embracing him.

"Often enough? Just that one time on the ship—in

Yokohama." He was puzzled by the turn in the conversation.

"One time?" the female voice laughed. "Why, Bill, have you really forgotten?"

Then he knew.

"Sarah?" he asked, returning her kiss reluctantly but feeling strange about embracing his naked sister on a bed. She was now a very desirable woman in full bloom, clinging to him and kissing him. "Oh, Bill . . . I've missed you so much—"

"I've missed you too, Sarah." He could feel heat rising in his loins. He had not exactly enjoyed a surfeit of women since first leaving San Diego for the Pacific. He tightened his arms around her, but when he felt her tongue lick his lips, he pushed away.

"God, Sarah, you're my sister."

"*Half*-sister," she said, refusing to let go.

"Just because of what we did when—well, it doesn't mean—"

"That's just what I was remembering, Bill," she said, reluctantly dropping her arms from around his neck and pulling the sheet over her breasts.

"I have to know, Bill." Excitement returned to her tone. "Why are you here? And how did you get here? We're in the middle of a war. What are you? A spy? You could be shot, you know."

"Not with a sister—"

"*Half*-sister."

"—who is the mistress of a Japanese general."

She chuckled. "I might turn you in myself. He'd like that."

"Where's Helma?"

"She's at her parents' home in Numazu. She went there for a couple of days to see if it was damaged. The B-29s bombed Numazu, you know."

"Who else is here?"

"No one. We're all alone, dear. There's no electricity and almost no food. So you might as well relax and lie down for the rest of the night. I promise I won't let you get any sleep."

"Now, Sarah. We can't—"

"No, silly. I'm not talking about that. I mean, I want to know everything that's happened since I last saw you."

"I don't think I can stay awake that long. I haven't slept in more than twenty-four hours."

"All right. If you fall asleep talking, I'll just cover you and let you sleep all day. This is Sunday anyway. I have to go out in the evening and—"

"To see General Doihara?" he asked, kicking off his shoes and shrugging out of his coat.

"Hmmm. You know an awful lot about me, don't you? Anyway, no one will bother you . . . at least, not until Helma gets back this evening."

"You think she can make it back by train . . . after the raid last night?"

"I don't know," Sarah said, pulling her brother—her *half* brother—down beside her and letting his head rest on her right arm. "Now, I'll ask the questions and you just answer them until you fall asleep, all right? And remember, I want to know everything."

Macneil was already feeling drowsy despite Sarah's warm naked body pressing against his left side. Her breasts—fuller than before—made him uneasy. "I've got a lot of questions to ask you, too, little sister."

"They may have to wait till Monday night. I'll be back then and you can ask to your heart's content—if Helma doesn't occupy all your time up here in bed."

"My God, you little devil. I keep sensing all these erotic undercurrents. What's happened?"

Her voice sobered. "I guess—I'm a different woman, Bill; I've changed a lot since Nathan—died."

"I was sorry to hear about that."

"Well, he's gone—but not forgotten, and your little half sister dances to different music now—although I'll never forget him."

"Well, we might as well get started."

"Start what?"

"Your interrogation, of course."

Sarah's voice was slower and low-pitched. "Hmmm . . . I'm . . . getting kind of sleepy, too. Maybe we should postpone it. I just want to lie here and drift off to sleep. I haven't felt so comfortable and safe in a long, long time—"

Bill Macneil had not changed his watch, Swiss-made, of course, to Tokyo time, but he figured it must be almost noon. He was still wearing his clothes, now twisted and rumpled, and he needed more sleep, but a sense of uneasiness had awakened him.

Quietly, so as not to disturb Sarah, he went to the east-facing window. The day was overcast, typical of the early rainy season in Tokyo. A pall of smoke hung over the center of the city. It was muggy, but the heat was nothing like the South Pacific combat arena. Tokyo would remain like this till the end of the *nyubai,* or rainy season, in July. Then a truly hot—but brief—session of summer weather would begin.

Nothing he saw was how he remembered it, nor how he expected it would be. One wing of his home was in ashes. To the east, only the homes of the Hashizuka and the Gocho families were standing.

He walked barefoot across the room to the southern view. Four houses were visible where eight or nine had stood. He had known all those people, played with their children, dated some of their daughters, swum and fished and hiked and fought with some of their sons. So many of them gone now, no doubt.

Macneil had not hated any of them, not even after Nanking. The ones he hated were the savages responsible for what happened to Ellen Wood—and those barbarians who had used a live American prisoner for bayonet practice in New Guinea. A connection between his Tokyo neighbors and the distant soldiers seemed, at best, tenuous.

He had yet to tour the other rooms, but it no longer seemed like the house he grew up in. The warmth, the comfort, the soul was gone. Only the shell remained, made of walls and floors and furniture, but the house was cold and cheerless, almost like a warehouse. The place smelled of ashes and mildew—and loneliness. Only two people lived in all the space where four years before, a dozen had shared an atmosphere of contentment and familial comfort.

The rest of the Moto-Azabu neighborhood was about the same. Quiet. Preternaturally so, as if waiting for another disaster to stalk its streets. No sounds of children playing. No cars or buses. No cries or horns from the omnipresent street vendors. No flutes from the blind masseuses. No clack-clack-clacking of the fire wardens.

Surely, a few people breathed inside those shells, but it was now a moribund neighborhood where everyone seemed to be waiting, resigned for the end.

Macneil knew he had come to hasten that end.

Bill had to talk seriously to Sarah about why he was in Tokyo.

How would she react? He wanted to find out about Japan's atom bomb program. Her patron, General Doihara, should know the answer, but could she inveigle him into telling her what he knew? And how dangerous would those inquiries, however subtle, be for Sarah?

Would she be willing to betray Doihara for her brother? Bill thought she would—or he would not be there. With all his being, he believed Sarah was American. Whatever camouflage she was wearing, whatever deception she was practicing, she was at heart American. He knew not what game she was playing—although he had a suspicion—but he was gambling she would be willing to help her country—and her brother.

He would try—and see.

If Sarah agreed, he would talk to Helma, but her involvement might not be needed. If Sarah agreed to help, and if she could get the information he needed from the commanding general of Japan's air forces, then that information would have to be transmitted to President Truman at flank speed.

The most certain way was for Macneil to deliver it in person, assuming he could get out of Japan in one piece. If not, he might have to rely on Helma Graf to relay his report—coded in an innocent-appearing letter—in the Swiss Embassy's diplomatic pouch to a relative of hers in Switzerland and from there to a prearranged address in Washington.

Macneil had two such letters ready. Neither said much of interest, but one would be understood to mean Japan would soon have atomic weapons ready for use against her enemies. The other would tell its recipient that as far as the writer could ascertain, Japan would not have atomic weapons ready for at least a year.

There was another way, an emergency communication channel, which would entail Helma's broadcasting one of two coded sentences at the end of her "messages from POWs" hour on Radio Tokyo. The first would purport to be from a Corp. Brent Holliman to his family in Billings, Montana; the other from Frank Vanzetti to his mother in Oak Park, Illinois. The first would mean this, the second that.

If the Japanese tried to confirm the source, which was unlikely, Helma would explain she must have misunderstood the prisoner's name.

All her broadcasts would be monitored and recorded until ATIS in Australia was told to desist. Macneil hoped he could persuade Helma to do this.

He turned back to the bed.

He needed more sleep. For a moment he was lost in contemplation of his sleeping sister—or *half*-sister, as she insisted on reminding him. God, she was lovely. Even with tangled hair and no makeup, she was a marvel of pristine beauty. The sheet covered her breasts—or almost. One nipple was peeking out impudently.

Sarah had the dignified poise of a highborn lady, although there was the lure of attractive abandon beneath the surface, and invitation—even demand—in her eyes. Little wonder, he reflected, that both a Japanese general and a colonel were smitten with her.

Raising the sheet gently, he gazed at the rest of her. Could he subject this splendid creature to the danger he had in mind?

For him this mission was a duty. He had to do it. And he wanted to. But to involve Sarah—and perhaps Helma—in this deadly exercise did not suit his sense of what was right.

Macneil settled himself on his side of the bed and sank into a much-needed sleep.

chapter 26

Sea of Japan
Tokyo, Japan
Late June 1945

In the United States, final preparations were being made to test an atomic weapon near Alamogordo, New Mexico. In Germany, after its disastrous defeat, the Americans, British, and Russians were competing to capture and kidnap Germany's nuclear scientists. In Japan, a light bomber had just taken off from an airfield in Matsue headed for Ullung Island in the Japan Sea. It carried an atom bomb considerably smaller than the one about to explode in New Mexico. Nonetheless, it was an atom bomb in every sense, and if its explosion fulfilled the expectations of Dr. Chinda Nishikawa, it would be the precursor of other bombs of much larger destructive capability.

The bomber was a Kawasaki Type 99, called Ki-88 by the Japanese air force and "Lily" by the Allies. Once over Ullung Island, it would turn directly north toward an uninhabited speck of land that was not even named on naval charts. It was formed by undersea volcanic action in 1939. The Japanese navy claimed it for a weapons testing ground, which it was about to become.

As soon as the speck was sighted, the pilot—a lieutenant named Terasaki—said to his copilot, "Have the weapon armed. I'm going down to 2,800 meters."

Two minutes later, the bombardier reported, "Ready to drop."

"Drop when ready," the pilot ordered. He could see houses on the island's coast and the dozen or so fishing craft assembled in a sheltered indentation. He knew both the houses and the boats were unoccupied and had been placed there only for this test.

"Don protective goggles," the pilot directed through the intercom.

"Bomb away!"

"Don't look down," the pilot said, turning his aircraft in a wide swing to the east.

Forty seconds later, the pilot said, "Grab hold of something." Eight seconds after that, the Lily bounced in a huge updraft. A brilliant light flashed through the sky. An explosion—louder than anything the crew had ever heard—temporarily deafened them.

The pilot violated his own order and looked back, then down. A column of smoke rose from the now invisible island. It was already beginning to mushroom.

Relieved, the pilot directed his navigator to set a course back to Matsue on the Japan Sea coast. Then he told his radioman, "Tell base the test was a success."

Pilot Terasaki felt a warm glow of self-congratulation and renewed hope for the future. He alone of the crew knew they had just dropped Japan's first atom bomb, that its spawn could well be the salvation of his beloved country.

In an apartment in Tokyo, Dr. Chinda Nishikawa was indulging in his only hobby: oil painting. Not many people knew about this aspect of the scientific genius. It would have seemed to many to be entirely out of character, which was why Nishikawa said little about it.

It was as if three-fourths of his mind was reserved for scientific speculation and the rest for his artistic predilections. At one time, he preferred to paint views of Mount Fuji in different climatic circumstances, but in recent years there had been little time for faring forth with easel and paint box to add another depiction of the Queen of Mountains to his collection. Instead, he had turned to nudes—specifically, his ex-geisha mistresses, like the one who was lounging on a futon before him.

"Open your legs more," he told this one, the fourth in his succession of concubines.

"*Hazukashii wa,*" she had replied, meaning she would be embarrassed. Seeing the dangerous glint in his eyes, she silently spread her legs.

Nishikawa grunted his acknowledgment.

Even so, he was not at all satisfied with this woman. Her breasts were too small and her thighs too heavy.

Like an overlay on a graph, he kept seeing that woman with the Chinese name as his model, superimposed over this unappealing ex-geisha.

He had not seen Lin Hsiao-mai, the granddaughter of the ex-ambassador, in the raw, of course, but was confident her breasts were full and arousing and her thighs slender and well-muscled, just the way he liked them. Often had he fantasized about this Eurasian woman since she escorted the six Jewish nuclear physicists from Shanghai to the Rikken Laboratory. He had dreamed about pushing in between her thighs while she loudly proclaimed to the heavens the ecstasy she was experiencing. He wanted her to claw his back and clutch at him with her vaginal muscles, the fabled *kinchaku* of Japanese sexual lore. Then, she would stuff a string of *juzu* beads far up his anus, to be yanked out at his instant of orgasm.

Nishikawa glanced at the clock on a bookshelf. He should know soon.

It had not been until early this year that Nishikawa had become aware that Lin Hsiao-mai was in Tokyo, working on Kenji Doihara's staff. Twice he had called her office inviting her to visit the Jewish scientists about whom she had seemed so concerned.

Lin Hsiao-mai had not risen to the bait, leaving Nishikawa gnawing his lips in frustration.

But he had a better idea. This time the lure was one she would not refuse.

He looked again at the clock.

If the test today was successful—and he believed it would be—he would no longer need the Shanghai Jews.

The Nuclear Weapons Committee of the Imperial General Staff had not yet been asked to decide the fate of the six. What the committee might decide was unclear, but nothing they did would surprise Nishikawa. If the Jews were no longer needed at Rikken, the committee might well send them to a detention camp in Japan.

Care had been taken to put the six to work in different departments at Rikken so no one of them would have an overall picture of the nuclear research and experimentation being conducted. Even so, Nishikawa doubted very strongly they would be sent back to their families in the Pootung Refugee Center in Shanghai.

Not unless Nishikawa insisted.

And that would be the lure that might enable him to snare the delectable Lin Hsiao-mai. He constructed in his imagination a conversation with that most desirable woman:

"I wonder if we could meet."

"I'm quite busy these days, Doctor Nishikawa. Is it urgent?"

"It concerns the six Jewish scientists you brought here from Shanghai."

"Oh?"

"I thought I might send them back to Pootung."

"Well, Doctor Nishikawa, perhaps we—"

"There are some other minor matters that need to be discussed, but I think you and I, by working together closely, can quite possibly effectuate their return."

"I see. Well, yes, of course, I believe I can find the time to call on you. Should I go to your office at Rikken?"

"A certain degree of confidentiality is needed, so it would be better if you could come to my living quarters for a private talk."

"I see . . . all right, I guess I could do that, if you'll tell me where to go."

Just then the telephone rang. It was his office at the lab.

"We've just heard from Matsue, *sensei*. Congratulations. The test was successful."

Nishikawa's heart leaped. He turned to the ex-geisha. "Put your kimono back on and go to the kitchen," he ordered. Already he was putting a fresh canvas on the easel. It would remain blank until the outlines of Lin Hsiao-mai's lovely nakedness began to take shape on it.

chapter 27

Tokyo, Japan
Late June 1945

Most of Japan was under the influence of the rainy season, poetically called the plum rains of summer. These were not the drenching downpours of Southeast Asia but slow drizzles that brought with them muggy overcast days, causing mildew to form on leather goods stored in dark closets. It also brought welcome respite from the B-29 visits because the pilots liked to see what they were destroying. But on those occasional clear days when the bombers could come back, Tokyoites looked with apprehension at the sky.

In Okinawa, American forces were mopping up after bringing a victorious end to the largest land battle of the Pacific war. More than 264,000 Americans, Japanese, and Okinawans had been killed.

Elsewhere, the United States was pushing ahead vigorously with its atomic bomb project while preparing for the two invasions of Japan: one aimed at southern Kyushu, the other at the Pacific beaches nearer Tokyo.

Radio Tokyo tried to keep up its regular broadcasting schedule but that was becoming increasingly hard. The staff had decreased, a few killed in raids, but more, fearful for their lives, had abandoned Tokyo for safer rural communities. It took many staffers so long to commute, they could spend only a few hours in the station each workday.

For all of Japan the average caloric intake was only 1,500 units a day. For those left in Tokyo, it was less. Baron Matsui, Captain Milmay, and the other military personnel at Radio Tokyo received the standard fare given the armed forces, which was largely inadequate. The baron tried to stay on his estate near Ashikaga as much as possible, so Helma seldom saw him. Helma was existing on her foreigner's rations and whatever the Swiss Embassy could distribute to its nationals, but it was far from enough. She found herself increasingly unsteady on her feet, moody, and despondent. In spirit and flesh, she was wasting away.

One night in late June, however, when Helma returned to Moto-Azabu from inspecting her parents' home—still undamaged—in Numazu, her outlook changed in a instant. In the kitchen, Bill Macneil was eating a meager meal by candlelight.

"Bill, oh, Bill! Thee are here! How did thee get here? Shouldn't thee be hiding in the basement?" She was in his arms kissing him frantically. "My love, my love! How I have missed thee!"

Bill knew his affection for the young Swiss woman had increased during the nearly four years of their separation, but he had not realized how delighted he would be to once again hold her in his arms. He had never put a name on his feelings for Helma but now, in the joyous moment of reunion, he could not call it anything but love. Without doubt he loved her mightily and believed sincerely that he always would.

"Helma," he said, holding her close, "I—love you. I know now that I do."

"And I love thee, darling."

"It'll soon be four years since we were last together," he told her between passionate kisses, "but I had all those letters from you and I heard your voice so often on Radio Tokyo that—well, I don't feel as if it's really been that long."

Tears were rolling down Helma's cheeks. She clutched him to her in a grip as strong as any man's. "I've dreamed so often of hearing thee say those words to me, Bill. I've never stopped loving thee. I've never dated another man. Thee has always been the only one in my heart."

Bill stood up from the table and blew out the candle. "Helma, do you mind? Can we go upstairs to my old room?"

"What about Sarah?"

"This is her night to be with General Doihara, I believe. Where do you sleep when she's here?"

Helma clung to his arm as they left the darkened dining room. "Usually she and I sleep in the same bed. There's another undamaged bedroom, but it's easier to make up one bed."

Climbing the stairs, Helma said, "I don't understand, dearest. Thee are here in Tokyo wearing civilian clothing. What has happened?"

Macneil laughed. "I'm one of your countrymen now, Helma. A Swiss national with a passport that reads Emil Grimm."

Helma Graf had a puzzled, worried look on her dimly seen

features. "Please, darling, don't upset me. I don't understand—tell me what has happened. Please."

"All right, all right. I'll tell thee—I mean, you—everything you want to know." He put his arm around her waist and half-carried Helma into the bedroom. "But there's something else I think we should attend to first, and it's something that can be done better if we're lying down."

"Oh, Bill. I can't wait. Hurry."

The next six days—in the enemy capital—were a honeymoon of sorts for Bill Macneil and Helma Graf. There wasn't much food but there were no air raids. Macneil thought how ironic it would be if he were killed by American bombs. Helma went to work three days of the six. On the others she stood in ration lines and called at the Swiss Embassy to pick up parcels of canned goods of Swiss origin. Macneil never left the house, and the couple tried to live by candlelight as much as possible. They did not want to arouse the curiosity of neighbors by revealing any unusual activity.

Sarah was seldom there, trying to spend as much time as she could with General Doihara. She cooked good meals for the general from the rations he brought to his living quarters, warmed his sake to just the right temperature, and entertained him on the futon with an agility that left him gasping.

Despite Sarah's adroit indirect inquiries, he had yet to say anything of the slightest interest to Macneil—or Harry Truman. Her brother kept urging her to greater efforts, but she protested she was doing everything she could short of blurting, "What's going on with Japan's atom bomb program?"

Sarah believed if her questions were too direct, her lover would—despite his intense infatuation—turn her over to the

Kempei-tai.

Macneil kept looking at the calendar hanging in the kitchen of the dark mansion. July 7 was creeping up at a rapid clip. That was when the submarine would surface off the west coast of Izu Peninsula watching for his flashlight. If there was none, it would come again on the 28th. After that, no more.

He considered boarding the submarine on the 7th—although the road to the Izu coast would be hard—leaving Harry Truman's mission in the hands of Sarah and Helma. Sarah would worm the answers out of Kenji Doihara somehow and Helma would broadcast them to Allied forces in the Pacific Theater. Perhaps Helma could use the coded letters and the diplomatic bag leaving the Swiss Embassy. This assumed the Swiss Embassy would still be standing and its diplomats had not fled Tokyo, if they were even alive.

While having those thoughts, Bill Macneil knew he could not abandon the field and turn the job over to the two people he loved more than any others. No, he would stay until he had what he needed. If he did not succeed and the submarine left without him, he would remain in hiding in Japan until the end of the war. If Truman used the "awesome weapon" he told Macneil about, it might all be over soon. If he did not, the greatest of all bloodbaths surely would ensue, and would make the slaughter on Okinawa seem like a pillow fight in a sorority house.

According to Helma and Sarah, the Japanese were already talking about mobilizing all "one hundred million" of their people, arming them with sharpened bamboo stakes. Every woman, child, and old man. Lining them up in the pine groves along the beaches. They would charge forth to hurl the *kichiku Eibei*, the British and American fiends, back into the sea. Imagine children running full-steam at a crack combat unit with sharp sticks. But it would not be beyond their capacity. Macneil knew his Japanese history and had read the story of the White Tiger Unit—the band of children who had fought adult samurai veterans to the death at the siege of White Crane Castle in the 1870s.

While waiting, Macneil tried to sedate his nerves by making love with the more than willing Helma as often as he could. After all, they had nearly four years of separation to make up for. When not lost in passionate embraces or recuperating in sleep, they told each other what had befallen them during those long months.

Little by little it became clear to Bill that Helma's love for the Japanese had changed to disappointment and dislike, although loathing might be a more accurate word for what she now felt. He knew something traumatic must have happened to occasion such a complete turnabout in her attitude, and finally he coaxed the explanation from her. The memory was so painful that Helma broke down.

"Oh, darling. It was awful. Just awful! That monster simply lopped the heads off of all of them. Then the little son-of-a-bitch strutted around as if he were proud of what he had done. And all the little monsters with him laughed and carried on as if they were at a party."

Macneil let her cry. He wished he could have cried when he saw the dead American with his head on his lap and his genitals in his mouth. But he also wished he could have wept when he heard about the American officer who urinated in the mouths of dead—or near-dead—Japanese whenever he could. He wished he could shed a river of tears for all mankind and for this bloody world he didn't ask to be born in, for all the anguish and tragic mortality that humanity entails.

At last Helma dried her eyes. "I guess thee can't believe I am the same Helma Graf thee said goodbye to on the freighter in Yokohama."

Bill probed her rib cage with a forefinger. "That afternoon you seduced me?"

"Was I too brazen? Did thee despise me, Bill?"

Macneil laughed. "No, I didn't mind being seduced. In fact, I relived that scene many times in the South Pacific, but I thought painting lipstick on your breasts and—your—you know—was a little too much."

"What if I do it again?"

"Try me."

With two days remaining before the first submarine rendezvous off Izu, Sarah Macneil hurried into the house at noon. She was so excited Macneil's heart bounded. He was certain she had the answers to his questions.

Sarah noticed his look of anticipation and tried to let him down gently. "I'm sorry, Bill. Truly I am." She was wearing a skirt and white blouse, and there was a thin film of perspiration on her forehead. "I haven't learned a thing. All Ken-san's time and thoughts are taken up with aircraft production and getting ready as many planes as possible to fly suicide missions against the American invasion forces. I'm sure he knows about the atom bombs, but there's absolutely no reason for him to say anything to me."

Dejected, Macneil slumped down in an easy chair in the living room. "Well, what's your news? You came in grinning like a Cheshire cat."

Her mobile features brightened again. "I'm taking the six Jews back to Shanghai, Bill. Today. On one of Ken-san's courier planes. Rikken Laboratory is through with them, and Dr. Nishikawa—I told you about him, didn't I?—called us and suggested we return the physicists to Pootung."

Sarah saw no reason to tell her brother about the interview with Chinda Nishikawa leading to his agreement to release them. It had been a close thing. It was obvious what the repellent gnome wanted. She had gone to his quarters mentally resigned to sharing her sexual largess if that was the only way to obtain the release of the six physicists, but she found a good excuse for postponing a final decision. The courier plane to Shanghai—few made the trip any more—was leaving that evening, which Nishikawa knew was true. She promised the father of Japan's atom bomb she would return to Tokyo within a few days so they could renew and deepen their acquaintance. It took considerable pleading and cajoling on Sarah's part, but she finally convinced him to let the Jews pack and deliver them to the airport in Atsugi in time for the evening departure.

"I was so worried about them, Bill. I was sure something terrible would be done to them. Now I can return them to their families and see how things are with all the others in Pootung."

"Are you still welcome in Shanghai? I thought—who was it, Colonel Ishihara?—had been shipped off to a combat command somewhere."

"That's part of the good news. I just learned he was found unfit for combat and was sent back to Shanghai." She glanced impishly at her brother. "I think he is still taken with me."

"Who wouldn't be? You're a hot little number, Chankoro."

She stuck out her tongue at her brother. "You know I don't like to be called 'Chink' and I don't think I like to be called a 'hot little number,' either. Just because I have to use my—ah, my undeniable charms now and then to save my people doesn't—"

"*Your* people?"

"You know who I mean. The Jews in Pootung."

"They're not your people, sister mine."

"They *are* my people. They are *my* Jews. If Nathan had lived, we would be married and I would have converted to Judaism. I promised Nathan to do my best for them. And besides, Bill, I love them. I really do. They're wonderful people."

"All right, all right, so they're your people. Are you coming back to Tokyo?"

"I haven't forgotten my promise to you, either. I'll try my best to get the information you want after I get back."

"Well, it looks as if I'll have to miss the first date for the submarine pickup."

"I'll be back as soon as I can," Sarah said, kissing him on the neck. "Hmm. Helma's such a lucky woman!" Her face bore a resolute expression.

"Now, Sarah, none of that."

"I must throw a few things in a bag. There's a car waiting for me outside. Oh, by the way, Bill. If anything should happen and I have to get in touch with you, the best way is through Ship."

"Shipton?"

"He's in the Special Attack Corps, you know—the poor guy. I'm so afraid he'll be sent on a suicide mission and—"

"If he's in the *Tokko-tai*, he's sure to go on one. Only one."

"That's why they get the best of everything; leave, parties, girls, sake. Letters to and from those boys are treated like communications from the emperor. So if I write to him at his air base—Kasumigaura?—the letter will be delivered the fastest way possible."

"And then?"

"He can bring word to you. His base is only a short way outside Tokyo."

"I hope it won't come to that. You'd better get back here as soon as you can and start working on your general again. That's the only way I'm going to find out what I want to know."

"I'll be back, and remember, I love you, Bill." She kissed him again and hurried off to pack.

CHAPTER 28

Tokyo, Japan
July 1945

July 7 had come—and gone.

It was the peak of the rainy season on the Great Kanto Plain, including Tokyo, Yokohama, and Kawasaki, with only occasional clear days.

Daily newspapers were reduced to about ten percent of their prewar circulation because of the shortage of newsprint. Home deliveries were a thing of the past, but Helma Graf would sometimes bring home often-read, bedraggled copies from Radio Tokyo. *Asahi* of the previous day informed her and Bill Macneil that today would be clear.

Over their morning tea, Bill urged her to stay home. "The B-29s will be over today, dearest. I'm sure they will. Look at that sky. There's some haze but not enough to stop them."

"I thank thee for worrying about me, Bill, but I must go. If they gave my job to someone else, how could I transmit thy message? I want very much to be part of this. My God is a vengeful god and His mills grind surely."

"If Sarah gets the information, I'll take it out of Japan myself—on the submarine. On the twenty-eighth."

But Helma was not to be dissuaded.

At 12:29 P.M., Macneil heard the air-raid sirens begin their chilling wail. By one o'clock, smoke was rising over Kawasaki, the city between Tokyo and Yokohama to the south.

Macneil wondered if the U.S. Air Force had decided to look for more rewarding targets than Tokyo, but he could not really believe that. According to Helma, most of the central business district of Marunouchi was unscathed, as were major parts of the Imperial Palace. Even on the high ground in Azabu, only about thirty percent of the homes had been razed. Within a hundred yards of the Macneil mansion, Bill could count twelve homes still standing—and eight empty spaces.

He feared their turn would come while he waited for Sarah to come back from Shanghai to start working on General Doihara again. He wanted to believe she would eventually learn what he needed to know, but would it be in time for him to meet the submarine on its second visit off Izu on the 28th?

Overcast skies again prevailed, and for a short while the great silver bombers stopped making their uninvited calls. With rising impatience, Macneil marked off day after day on the calendar in the kitchen. Helma reported only about a third of the foreign broadcast staff at Radio Tokyo was coming to work. Baron Matsui had assembled everyone and said he would not blame them if they evacuated to a country district. Many took him at his word, so the number appearing for work decreased day to day. Even the baron was absent more often than he was present.

Just when Bill Macneil was about to give up on Sarah, his half brother Shipton, now Flying Officer Wataru Miyoshi—used his own key to open the front door and climbed the stairs to the second floor. Bill met him on the landing. They embraced and yelled and pounded each other.

"By damn, Ship, I can't tell you how glad I am to see you. Why, you're as tall as I am. Taller, I believe."

There were tears in Shipton's eyes. He gulped and said huskily, "This war has made a mess of our lives, hasn't it, Bill?"

Soberly, Bill replied. "It sure as hell has. Why, you're an officer in the Special Attack Corps and I'm an American army officer, and we should be trying our best to kill each other right now."

"We could never fight each other, could we?"

"No, of course we couldn't. Let's find a place to sit down and get caught up."

"All right, but let me take a leak first."

"And, by the way, what the bloody hell are you doing in a getup like that? I always figured you to be the most loyal American of us all."

Shipton stopped and looked out one of the windows. "I know, Bill, but don't you see? I had to . . . to stay with Mother."

"That didn't work out, did it? She's down in Nagasaki and you're on a base outside Tokyo. And what's with this anyway?" Bill pointed to the Special Attack Corps badge on his half-brother's jacket.

"I didn't ask for that. They just assigned me to the *Tokko-tai*."

After two and a half hours of conversation, the pair still had not exhausted all they wanted to ask each other. Suddenly, Shipton snapped his fingers. "I almost forgot the main reason I'm here. I got this letter from Sis and I guess it must be for you. I don't understand it."

Most of Sarah's letter was the kind of message a sister would write to a brother, but the part that puzzled Shipton read,

> "On the plane back to Shanghai, I talked to a very interesting group of six men who knew all about the kind of dogs we are trying to breed. Back home I found that one of our dogs had already whelped a pure black puppy that is in good shape. How I wish I could tell our brother about this. You know how he loved dogs. The other bitch should litter in October and I bet she'll give us five or six of the cute little devils.
>
> P.S. There's no longer any reason for me to return to Tokyo so I'll stay right where I am for a while. I have all these 'animals' to look after. They really need me, you know. I'm sure our brother would understand if only I could tell him."

Macneil was filled with pleasure and excitement. He knew just what Sarah was trying to tell him. The Japanese had successfully tested one atomic weapon and would have five or six more ready by October. The six German-Jews had learned much more while working in the Rikken Laboratory than Chinda Nishikawa ever dreamed they would.

At first he was disappointed to learn she would not be coming back to Tokyo, but on reflection he realized that was better.

Shanghai was a far safer place at this stage of the war.

When Helma Graf returned from Radio Tokyo in the late afternoon, the trio had a celebratory reunion with their father's Scotch. He had concealed six bottles with the cash he had stashed before leaving Japan. Then Shipton had to return to his base on the shores of Lake Kasumigaura.

Bill still had not told his half brother the true reason for his being in Tokyo, but Shipton must have had a fairly good idea. He told Bill, "Maybe I can help you in whatever you're doing."

"I'll keep it in mind. Will we see you again?"

"I get a week's leave soon."

"A whole week? With the war going the way it is?"

"It's my final leave. All of us get one week just before we go on what they like to call our 'glorious mission.' "

"My God, Ship! Are they really going to send you out alone against a battleship or aircraft carrier?"

Shipton nodded miserably. "But I promise you, Bill. I'll only dive my plane into an empty stretch of ocean."

"But what about *you*, Ship? Can't you get out?"

"You know I can't."

Bill was silent for a moment. "Well, there might be a way. Tell me, when does your leave start?"

"I have some flexibility, but I have to take it before the end of this month."

"All right. Start your leave on the 23rd of July and come here first. Where will your leave orders read?"

"Nagasaki. I wanted to see Mother."

"I'll be waiting here for you on the 23rd and we'll work something out. I've got an idea about how we can get you out of this."

"You'd better tell me what you have in mind."

"Time for that later. You just be here with your leave orders in hand on the 23rd."

Shipton got up to leave.

"One more thing," Bill said. "If I'm not here, go to Helma's place in Numazu. It's on the way to Nagasaki. You know where the house is, don't you? I may be there. Or she can tell you where I am."

"Won't she be in Tokyo?"

"I'm trying to persuade her to get out of Tokyo. There may be a lot more damage done to this city and I don't want her here."

Shipton studied his brother's face carefully. "There's something going on, isn't there?"

"There sure as hell is, Ship, and it would be extremely dangerous if you knew. Just do as I say and there's a chance I can solve all our problems. If I don't, we may not be alive to worry anyway."

Before Ship left, his half brother made him dig his American passport out of a trunk in the basement.

The following day was clear again and everyone knew what that meant. It was sure to be Tokyo—or what remained of the capital city—this time. Macneil made Helma leave early for Numazu. He did not want them to travel together. If he were suspected and caught in her company, she would certainly be implicated, and he had to avoid that. He would find some way to reach her home in Numazu alone and from there, by July 28, to the tiny inlet of Heda on the west coast of the Izu Peninsula, just down the coast.

Warily, Macneil watched the eastern sky from a second-floor window while Helma was packing.

"I don't think I should go, Bill."

"Do you want to help me get on that submarine?"

"Of course."

"Then go," he said. "And something else, dear. Take Ship's passport. And pack one of his suits in your bag. A civilian suit. He must have clothes somewhere in the house."

"I know where they are. When will I see thee?" She was almost in tears.

"I'll try to reach Numazu later today."

She ran to him and threw her arms around his neck. "Maybe we should just stay here till the 26th or even the 27th."

"No, Helma. I have a premonition the B-29s will be including Azabu in their drop zone this time."

CHAPTER 29

Tokyo, Japan
July 16, 1945

Major Bill Macneil cursed the clear skies—and waited.

The Azabu neighborhood and, in fact, all of Minato ward also waited in dreading anticipation. They knew their turn would come. Too much of this sector of Tokyo still stood. General Curtis LeMay's bombardiers would not forget them. It was as if tens of thousands of people were holding their breaths, trying to will the inexorable hands of the clock from moving forward.

But move forward they did. At 1:13 P.M. the air-raid sirens began their doleful wail. Thirteen minutes later the awesome phalanxes of B-29s appeared on the eastern horizon. Relentlessly they marched on directly at the Macneil mansion and its neighbors in Azabu. They flew low, impudently insouciant to the anti-aircraft fire of the enfeebled Japanese air defenses. No fighters rose to challenge them today. General Doihara's air force still had thousands of aircraft, but not much fuel, and he was hoarding both gasoline and planes for the invasion sure to come.

Macneil stood at the window of his second-floor bedroom and cheered the oncoming waves. Come on, you bastards! he thought. Bomb the shit out of them. Never mind me. One more good pounding and maybe the whole damn country will call it quits.

But even as he had the thought, Macneil knew in his heart the Japanese would not quit. He hated them and at the same time admired them for that. No, sir. They were not going to quit. No matter what.

Many of his countrymen called that stubbornness "fanaticism," but Macneil knew it for what it was: incredible courage and stoicism in the face of extreme danger.

The bomb explosions were coming nearer, sounding like the thundering footsteps of a leviathan tramping forward to attack. Fascinated, Macneil could not move. He knew he should seek shelter, but where could he find safety from incendiaries? He made sure his Swiss passport and Japanese currency were secure in their waterproof pouch in his trousers pocket, then walked to the front of the mansion. He stood at a window where he could see the street outside the gate.

Five neighborhood women stood next to the water tank holding buckets. All wore the padded jackets that were regulation garb for fire fighting. Macneil knew them all from his boyhood. One, Mrs. Sasakawa, had a baby strapped to her back, a smaller padded jacket wrapped around the infant.

Macneil shook his head sadly. This was how Japan proposed to fend off those mighty B-29s swarming overhead, the roar of their engines reverberating through the house and shaking the walls. Five women—one burdened by a baby—were going to fight off the devastation of the 21st Bomber Command. Had it not been so pitiable, it would have been hilarious. Macneil didn't know whether to laugh or cry.

Before he could do either, a stick of incendiaries dropped on the neighborhood. Other houses within Macneil's vision were hit. The heavy roof tiles afforded some protection from the flames, but the walls were wooden. If a tree began to burn, the fire quickly spread to the wooden sides of the house.

Half the houses within his sight quickly caught fire. Gallantly, the female fire wardens sprang to their tasks. Back and forth they sped, tossing their piteous pails of water first at this conflagration, then at that. It was like midgets pissing on the flames of Hades. The fire gods laughed at their feeble thimblefuls and challenged the women to bring more.

Suddenly, Macneil saw that the agile Mrs. Sasakawa, whose home was only 40 yards down the other side of the street, was running back and forth, unaware the padded jacket wrapped around the baby on her back was blazing.

If the infant did not already feel the heat of the flames, it would soon. When it did, it was sure to begin to cry, but would Mrs. Sasakawa recognize the reason for her child's distress? Macneil knew something had to be done.

Running downstairs, he flung open the front door and dashed into the street, vaguely aware that part of his own home was burning. This was the first time he had ventured outdoors since parachuting onto Mount Takao.

"*Sasakawa-san!*" he shouted, "*Akachan ni hi ga tsuite iru yo.*" ("Mrs. Sasakawa! Your baby is on fire!")

Pulling off her *obi* and tearing the padded jacket away from the infant, Macneil grabbed the bucket of water from the mother and threw its contents on the baby, whose clothes were smoldering in places, but he was in time to save it from serious burns.

At that instant, the roof of the burning house across the narrow street collapsed, its heavy tiles sliding onto Macneil. Weighing the standard twelve pounds each, three of them struck Macneil in succession: two hitting his head, the other, his right shoulder.

Where before he had heard the roar of the bombers overhead, the crackling of the flames, and the wham-wham of bursting incendiaries, a sound burst inside Macneil's head that drowned out all else, filling his skull and forcing its way out his nose and mouth and ears. It broke through tissue and bone. He was aware of nothing else. Nothing at all.

First there was the pain. Pounding pain. Then sightlessness. Was he blind or merely unable to open his eyelids? He could not raise his hands to feel his eyes. That required an effort far beyond him. He gave up—and sank into blackness again.

Macneil's next awareness was a phantasmagoria of sounds. Female voices were speaking Japanese, becoming louder, then fading. He should have understood what they were saying, but pain made individual words indistinguishable.

He knew he was being tended to. He could feel wet cloths being rubbed on this part and that of his body. He felt his head being gently lifted and cloth wrapped around it. His lips were forced open and liquid allowed to flow in by the spoonful. The coolness in his parched throat was a pleasure almost beyond description. From time to time he was rolled from one side to the other for mysterious purposes. He groaned whenever his weight came to bear on his right shoulder.

Drifting in and out of consciousness, he realized time must be passing, time in large measure, and that worried him, but he could not think why.

At last, his thoughts began to assume a semblance of order. Three questions loomed above all others: Where am I? What is the date? How bad are my injuries?

He knew he had an urgent reason to be up and on his way to some destination, but exactly where and why had yet to become clear.

Much that was being said around him seemed to be idle chatter, but occasionally his ears grasped a phrase or sentence that answered, at least in part, what he wanted to know.

"We really should try to call a doctor, you know."

"Don't be silly. Even if we found one alive, how could we explain an American being here?"

"You're sure this is Bill Macneil, not Shipton?"

"Of course. I've known him since he was born."

"But why does he carry this Swiss passport?"

"Maybe he became Swiss to marry Helma Graf."

"But that would not explain the name Emil Grimm."

"The Hashimoto's daughter, Midori, looked in on him yesterday. She thinks he has a concussion, but no broken bones."

"What does she know?"

"She's a nurse, isn't she?"

"Oh? I didn't know that. A real nurse?"

"Well, she had some kind of training at the Red Cross Hospital."

"She did a good job with these bandages. His whole head is wrapped neatly."

"What I'd like to know is: What are we going to do with him?"

"Whether he's Swiss or American, we should report him to the police, shouldn't we?"

"Don't you dare. He's like a member of my family."

"Then we're agreed? We keep him here until he's better. Then we'll see what he wants to do."

"I hope there are no more air raids."

"We'll take turns sitting up with him, all right? Eight hours each. Mrs. Uno first and then Mrs. Tanikawa. And Sachie-san. She's fifteen and can do her share."

"I wish some of the men—"

"What men?" (Laughter.)

"How's your baby, Mrs. Sasakawa?"

"The burns are healing. You know, Bill-san saved her life. I'll be forever grateful to him—"

"The police came around yesterday."

"What for?"

"They were picking up those leaflets the Americans dropped."

"I didn't read one."

"I did. The Americans were telling us to get out of the big cities. Some of the cities will be destroyed, they said." (Bitter laughter.)

"How can you destroy something that's already destroyed?"

"Besides, where would we go?"

"And how would we get there?"

"Some of the trains still run."

"Yes, but they're too crowded to get aboard."

"I wonder what the Americans would think if they knew they were bombing this American." Macneil felt an affectionate pat on his left shoulder.

"If only Sarah and little Shipton were here."

"Well, they're not and we just have to do the best we can. Bill-san was like a brother to my son Hisaya."

"Have you heard from Hisaya?"

A long silence—and then, "He was on Okinawa."

On July 23, Flying Officer Wataru Miyoshi appeared in the devastated neighborhood. After seeing his home burned to the ground, he inquired at the neighboring houses. At one he was quickly ushered inside and taken to Bill Macneil's room.

Bill Macneil was able to stand and stagger about, and his sight was returning.

"You look like a damned Egyptian mummy," Shipton said, shaking his head.

"Are the trains running to Numazu, Ship?"

"The tracks between Shinagawa and Tokyo Central are torn up, but if we can reach Shinagawa, we can get aboard something or the other there."

"How can we get to Shinagawa?"

"I'll go get a rickshaw."

"I'll be dressed and ready when you get back." He turned and embraced the Japanese women in the room one by one. They tittered in embarrassment.

"I have to go, but I'll be back when the war is over. I'll see to it you are all repaid for your kindness."

"Take care of yourself, Bill-san," they chorused. "Give our best to your family."

Macneil felt almost as close to these women as he did to his own family. They had risked their lives to protect him. They were the same people he remembered from his boyhood: untiring in their compassion and efforts for the sake of others.

Were these the ones he was condemning to fiery deaths?

CHAPTER 30

Numazu, Japan
Heda, Japan
July 24-28, 1945

The medium-size city of Numazu lay 76.5 miles southwest of Tokyo. To get there by train took one hour and forty-four minutes on a limited express in good times, but these were not good times. Indeed, these were the worst of times. The rails crossed the base of the Izu Peninsula, with the ever-magnificent Mount Fuji looming large on the right hand, then entered the town of Mishima. From there they proceeded to Numazu on the coast.

The Macneil brothers changed trains twice. Once, they were forced to detrain at Oiso, walking three miles along bomb-damaged track to another train waiting at the beginning of a stretch of undamaged track. From Odawara on across the Izu Peninsula the progress was rapid because the train passed through many tunnels that protected the rail lines from harm. Even so, the two did not arrive at Numazu Station until late on the evening of July

24. The submarine was due off Heda on July 28.

No one had questioned or attempted to stop the brothers for any cause. Shipton's uniform and his badge identifying him as a member of the sure-to-die Special Attack Corps earned him salutes even from higher-ranking officers. With pitying looks, ordinary civilian passengers, of whom there were only a few, often whispered behind their hands to each other. Perhaps, they were saying how sad it was to see the flower of Japan's youth sacrifice their lives so the empire might flourish for "10,000 years."

The slightly bloodstained cloth around Bill Macneil's head was a prime example of the Japanese tendency toward excessive bandaging. Only his eyes, nose, and mouth were visible, and he carried his gauze face mask in a jacket pocket should even more concealment become advisable. That he was obviously injured and being escorted by one of the young *gun-shin,* or war-gods, of the air force was enough to insure his inviolability.

An hour after leaving the train, the pair reached the home of Helma Graf's parents, on the edge of Sembonhama Park. The house was dark because residential electricity was cut off at eight o'clock. The street was deserted.

Bill Macneil identified the house as the Graf residence by the sign in *kana* at the gate. It had not been damaged, although that could not be said for the rest of the neighborhood. He knocked softly, not wanting to arouse the curiosity of the neighbors. Eventually, Helma appeared and immediately drew both the men into the interior.

"Shipton!" she cried, "Is this Bill?" Assured it was, she threw her arms around him, careful not to touch his head. "Oh, dearest, what has happened to thee? Come in, come in. Here, I'll light a candle. How bad is thy wound, dearest?"

The morning of July 28, Numazu was shrouded in rain. Thunder in the west signaled the approaching close of the rainy season.

Although he no longer needed it, the bandage around Bill Macneil's head was left in place. His right shoulder pained him now and then, but he had regained most of the use of his right arm.

At noon, Helma Graf hurried back into the small house. "I've got it," she cried, lifting a piece of paper.

"The ferry schedule," she explained. "There's one leaving at five-thirty, and it reaches Heda at eight. That will surely give thee enough time, won't it?"

Bill Macneil nodded.

"Oh, Bill. A pair of policemen are on foot patrol in the neighborhood. They asked if I was all right."

Bill cast a questioning glance at her.

"Oh, they know me. I usually go to the police box when I leave for Tokyo and tell them no one will be here for a while. They sort of look after the place for me."

"If they'll just leave us alone for a few more hours, we'll be all right."

"Why do thee say that?" she asked.

"Because we will all be gone, that's why."

She was indignant. "Well, *I* won't be. I'll be right here, and I may need their help if the bombers come back."

"Wha—aat? You're not going with us?"

"I changed my mind, Bill. Last night, in fact."

"You *are* going with us, Helma!" Bill was nearly shouting. "Of course you're going. We won't leave without you."

Helma approached Bill and pulled his lips to hers. "Listen to me, dearest. I can't swim. Not a stroke. I'd sink like a hammer."

"That doesn't matter. Ship and I—we'd carry you between us. We'd—"

"For two hundred yards or more? Thee with an injured shoulder and half blind? Don't be silly. Besides, there are probably sharks out there." Her face took on a resolute expression. "But thee had better come back here and get me when the war's over. Promise?"

"You will stay here in Numazu?"

"The Swiss Embassy in Tokyo has been destroyed and most of the Swiss have evacuated to Karuizawa, but this is my home. I like it here and I might as well be here as in Karuizawa."

"Jesus, Helma—"

"Don't thee dare blaspheme, Bill Macneil."

"Why did you wait till the last minute?"

"So thee would not be able to change my mind."

Macneil fumed and sputtered and stalked around the room, but to no avail.

"You don't have any food," Macneil pointed out persuasively.

"I still have cash from what your father hid in the Tokyo house. I can get what I need on the black market. You can buy anything if you have enough money. And maybe I'll just spend my time fishing."

"Damn! Ship, did you hear that? This crazy woman has decided not to go with us."

Shipton smiled sheepishly. "I can kinda understand her feelings, Bill. There *are* sharks out there, you know. We were warned about them in training."

Macneil shook his head in disgust. "Anyway, you and I don't

have any choice."

"Actually, I do have a choice, you know."

"What? Are you going to back out, too? You've already over-stayed your leave, haven't you? Isn't that desertion?"

"Take it easy, Bill. I may desert the Special Attack Corps but not you. I'm going with you, although I'll be praying the sharks don't eat us."

"Baloney. The damn sharks are the least of our problems. Anyway, you might as well get ready. Wear your civilian clothes and put your American passport in that waterproof pouch. I'll give you a letter to put in the pouch, too. It will be addressed to President Truman, and you be damn sure to get it to him as soon as you can."

"*Me*? What about you?"

"That's just in case something happens to me between the shore and the sub. And Helma, after we are gone, burn Ship's uniform and the leave orders in his pocket."

Helma Graf was on the verge of tears when Macneil led her into one of the bedrooms to bid her a proper farewell.

The open-sided ferryboat left Numazu harbor in the rain, its diesel engine chugging steadily. Only eleven of the thirty-six seats were filled. The captain and two sailors were aboard, but apparently had no authority to examine any documents other than tickets. Shipton was, to be sure, in a highly vulnerable position since he carried no I.D. but a United States passport, long out-dated. But both the brothers spoke native-quality Japanese, and Shipton looked somewhat Japanese, at least more than his sister Sarah did. Bill's blond looks were mostly concealed under his head bandage and behind the gauze mask he wore once again.

When the ferry docked in Heda down the Izu coast, the other disembarking passengers quickly disappeared into the night. In the tiny town were fewer than a hundred dwellings, and they quickly swallowed the arrivals from Numazu, except for the Macneils. Bill and Ship walked slowly west to the edge of the quiet town. When no one was in sight, they hurried along the rocky shore to the point Bill Macneil had marked with an X on a map for the submarine commander.

Once there, they impatiently awaited the appointed hour.

At ten sharp, Shipton sighted the flashing light on the submarine. Exuberantly, Bill signaled back. When his signal was acknowledged, he tossed the flashlight into the sea, then followed it himself, with his brother in tow.

"One last thing," Bill said. "Don't say anything to anyone about your having been in the Special Attack Corps. Just pretend it never happened. Say you were an American citizen caught in Japan by the war. Say the Japanese let you alone because, until very recently, you were a minor. Got it?"

"Yeah, Bill."

"If it ever becomes an issue—though I don't think it will, I'll talk to the president about it. He'll owe me one hell of a big one when I get back to Washington."

Shoulder to shoulder, the brothers began swimming in long, sure strokes toward the American sub.

Chapter 31

Across the Pacific and on to
Washington, D.C.
July 29—August 6, 1945

The Macneils' submarine was delayed reaching Saipan.

A Japanese destroyer located the American submersible on its sonar off Miyake-jima. The destroyer was part of the defensive screen being thrown around the home islands. The submarine was forced to run at minimum speed and maximum depth to avoid the deluge of depth bombs.

Just when the first destroyer seemed to have exhausted its supply of depth bombs, a second took its place and resumed the chase.

"I told you, sharks would be the least of your worries." Bill said to his brother as the submarine shivered from the explosions.

"I think I prefer the sharks," Ship said. "When will we reach Saipan?"

"At this pace, next year."

"Seriously."

"I have no idea, but there's one fellow in Washington who is certain to be damned unhappy about the delay."

When the submarine at last docked at the makeshift pier on Saipan, a delegation of high-ranking officers was there to meet Bill Macneil. A three-stripe admiral took him by the elbow and introduced him to a two-star general with wings over his left pocket.

"This is the officer all the fuss is about," the admiral said.

"My God, Major," the air force general said. "Harry Truman has been screaming for days. Whatever you and he have cooked up between you, I don't think I want to know about it."

"Good," Bill said. "I couldn't tell you anyway."

"Let's go. We have a plane waiting."

"Don't I get to shower and eat something?"

"No, you don't. We've got our fastest fighter plane waiting and—"

"*Fighter* plane?"

"We had an extra seat built in. We'll fly you to Wake and Johnson, then Honolulu and San Francisco and on across the U.S. Only a few minutes at each stop for re-fueling."

"I've got to use a toilet, General."

"I'll give you ten minutes. No more."

"And about my brother here—"

"Yes?"

"He's an American citizen who got caught by the war in Japan. Couldn't get out. How about seeing to it he gets to San Francisco and calls our father up in Oregon?"

The air force general looked dubious, but the admiral, who outranked him, intervened. "Don't worry, Major. We'll get him there and even give him a nickel for the phone call. Any great hurry to get him to Oregon?"

"Not nearly as much as there is to get me to Washington," Bill said. "And thanks."

Bill Macneil shed the jacket of his Swiss-made suit, visited the toilet, then said goodbye to his brother.

"Ship, I hate to think what could have happened if we hadn't got you out of there."

"Thanks, old pal. You always were the one I could depend on—that *all* of us could depend on, in fact."

"Now it's Sarah and your mother and Helma we have to worry about. I only hope our luck holds."

Before climbing into the rear cockpit of the fighter, Macneil paused to let the admiral brief him on recent developments.

"The Jap prime minister—what's his name?"

"He's an admiral. Kantaro Suzuki," Bill replied. "Not a bad fellow, I hear. My father knew him, though I didn't."

"Anyway, he announced Japan would reject the terms of the Potsdam Declaration."

"Hmmm. That doesn't sound like old man Suzuki. I wish I knew what language he used."

"I've got a copy of the bulletin right here," he said, pulling it out of a pocket. "It just came in this morning."

With one foot on the ladder to the cockpit where his pilot waited, Macneil ran his eyes down the single sheet of yellow communications paper.

"Damn!" he grated. "Look at this, Admiral. The prime minister used the word '*mokusatsu*' and some idiot translated that as 'to reject with silent contempt.' "

"Is that wrong?"

"It sure as hell isn't right, sir. *Mokusatsu* has a complex meaning, but to me it says the Japanese want more time to ponder their reply to the Potsdam terms."

"Is that important?"

"I think it is. If Truman assumes Japan has contemptuously rejected the peace proposal, he'll just push ahead with the war. Full speed."

"Would it do any good if I sent a message to the navy chief of staff?"

"I don't know, sir. I think I had better get back to Washington just as soon as possible. Maybe I can straighten this out there—if it's not too late."

It was late the next day when Major Bill Macneil reported to military intelligence headquarters in Washington. Lights were still burning in some of the offices. The duty officer, a captain, looked up inquiringly as Macneil, still in civilian clothes, approached.

"I'm Major William Macneil. I came straight from the airport."

The captain leaped to his feet. "Thank God you're here, Major. Every man and his dog in this city has been waiting for you. Sit down a minute, sir. Over there. I'll call the White House."

A few minutes later he walked over to where Macneil was stewing impatiently. "The president is in a cabinet meeting, Major. I got through to a military aide, though, and he managed to have a word with the president. He says you're to report first thing tomorrow."

That seemed odd to Macneil. "I thought he'd want to see me immediately."

"To tell you the truth, I thought so, too, Major—considering the ruckus they have been raising. Do you have a place to stay for tonight?"

"Not yet."

"We have some spare bunks here in headquarters, if you don't mind."

"That would be fine. I'll get dinner somewhere and then take a turn around the block. May I leave my bag here?"

"Certainly—and another thing. You still have that Swiss passport?"

Macneil nodded.

"Hold on to it for tonight, sir. We'll give you back your regular I.D. tomorrow."

Macneil was tired and sleepy but he wanted to eat dinner. He also wanted to decide what to tell the president tomorrow, the sixth day of August. He decided to walk over to Pennsylvania Avenue and find a restaurant. Perhaps the stroll would clear his head.

Macneil had known almost from the beginning the "awesome weapon" President Truman had told him about had to be an atom bomb. It meant the United States was building atomic weapons, and the president had to decide whether to use them against Japan, since Germany was out of the war.

Well, Japan had tested one atom bomb, according to Sarah Macneil, and would have others ready in the fall. If he told Harry Truman that, the president would, almost without doubt, order the U.S. to make a preemptive strike.

On the other hand, if he submitted to his commander-in-chief an evasive report, it would be a toss-up, perhaps, as to what Truman would do.

If it were a straightforward question as to whether, say, one hundred thousand Americans should be slaughtered on the invasion beaches or one hundred thousand Japanese should be incinerated, Macneil's decision would not confront him with any ethical dilemma. After all, he was a loyal American. Nevertheless, he could not forget those five pathetic Japanese housewives futilely running back and forth with their little pails of water to fling on the raging fires. And one with a baby strapped to her back. Nor would he ever forget those same neighborhood women who nursed him back to health and protected him at enormous risk to themselves.

Steadfast, compassionate little women they were, who had known and loved him when he was a child, ignoring his foreign blood. He did not know which of Japan's cities would be atombombed, but Tokyo was surely high on the list. Could he repay their kindness by aiding and abetting their obliteration?

At the back of his mind was the idea that Truman might be persuaded to set aside, for a while, reliance on atomic weapons or a full-scale invasion. The U.S. could blockade the entire enemy archipelago and let hunger do its work. Starvation and disease could be very effective, although not exactly a humanitarian alternative.

There was also the matter of Prime Minister Suzuki's "rejection" of the Potsdam Declaration. He would try to tell the president that Suzuki's message in its original Japanese had not been the flat rejection the State Department had judged it.

Anyway, the president probably would not listen to Macneil's proposals. Why should he? He had ordered Macneil to learn what he could about the status of atomic weapon development in Japan. He had said nothing about a strategy for bringing Japan to its knees.

At length, over coffee, Bill Macneil decided what he would tell Truman. Having made up his mind, he slept well.

chapter 32

Washington, D.C.
August 6, 1945

Major Bill Macneil went through three identity verifications on his way to meet President Truman.

After that, he waited an hour and fifteen minutes, sensing a strong current of excitement in the outer offices. The military officers, politicians, and bureaucrats were moving faster and looking even more harried than he remembered. Several carried reports they shoved in each other's faces with triumphant looks.

Clearly, something of utmost importance had happened, and Macneil felt he was the only one who did not know what it was.

At last, he determined to find out. He broke in on the dialog of the white receptionist and a pretty black woman standing at her side.

"Excuse me, but—"

"I'm sorry, Major, but you haven't been called yet."

Macneil smiled and leaned toward her. "It's not that. I just wondered—can you tell me what all the excitement is about? I think everyone but me must know."

"Oh, you haven't heard?"

"Heard what?"

"We've dropped a bomb on Japan."

I know that, Sis, Macneil thought. We've dropped about fifty thousand bombs on Japan and some of them damned near hit me.

The pretty black woman added, "It was some kind of special bomb, Major. What did the paper say: an atomal bomb?"

"An atom bomb?"

"That's it, sir. An *atom* bomb. On a place called Shirashima, I think."

"You probably mean Hiroshima," Macneil corrected. My God, he thought. Truman must have decided not to wait. He went ahead and used it.

Macneil felt a tremendous weight lift from his spirits. What he was going to tell the president no longer mattered. It was all a *fait accompli*.

Another half hour passed before he was summoned into Truman's presence. The president looked pretty much as Macneil remembered him, except he may have been more harassed. Macneil realized again how short the man was. He was dressed in a light-gray double-breasted suit with a red-and-blue bow tie. A half dozen aides surrounded the man from Missouri, all trying to catch his attention with one urgent matter or the other.

"Major Macneil," Truman said, holding out his hand briskly. The president's voice was high, abrasive, and flat. One knew this man's origins—the Midwest—quickly. "I guess you've heard?"

"Yes, sir."

"I put you to a lot of trouble for nothing, didn't I?"

You sure as hell did, you bastard, Macneil wanted to say but, of course, did not.

"Not that it matters now, but what did you find out? Do the Japs have the bomb?"

"Yes, sir, they do. They have tested one successfully and could have a handful more ready before our invasion in the fall."

"They knew about the invasion plans, did they?"

"Yes, sir." It did not matter any longer what Macneil told Harry Truman. America had atomized Hiroshima and if Tokyo was next, Macneil would bear none of the blame.

Truman took Macneil by the elbow and walked him to a far corner of the office. "I won't ask you what you had to do to obtain that information, but I want you to know how much I appreciate what you've done. Your report relieves me of a heavy burden, Major. The Japanese prime minister rejected the Potsdam terms, you know. I might have negotiated a little more, but when I read the wording of his rejection, I hit the roof."

"The wording, sir?"

"That Jap word—I can't remember it—that our translators said meant, 'to reject with silent contempt'. The little son-of-a-bitch. He rejects a proposal from me with silent contempt? That was just too much to stomach."

"Mister President," Macneil interrupted, "I don't think the prime minister meant what you say he meant. The word *mokusatsu* is a difficult word to translate, and I think you might have asked for a clarification."

Truman looked at Macneil in surprise. "Oh? Well, I don't know. I was told you know the Jap language like a native, and it wouldn't be the first time my experts—Washington is crawling with the bastards—were wrong, but in this case it's all academic. Whatever the prime minister meant, he's got the message now: The city of Hiroshima almost totally destroyed and maybe one or two hundred thousand Japs burned to death. And if I don't get a more polite answer from him in a day or so, I might send him another message."

"You'll drop another bomb?"

The president chuckled archly. "I just might, Major."

He might get hit on the head for speaking up, but Macneil felt he had earned the right to say something. "I hope it won't be Tokyo, sir."

"Why not?"

"As you know, I was just there and the city is already devastated. You would be wasting a bomb."

"We'll see," the president mused. "Anyway, your report justifies the decision I made. If I had not ordered the use of our bomb, they would have used theirs on our boys in November. We know they've got about 2000 kamikaze aircraft camouflaged or under trees on Kyushu. Just imagine the bloodbath that would take place with that many kamikazes and maybe five atom bombs—even small ones."

"There may have been another way, Mr. President."

Truman looked at Macneil sharply. "You mean a blockade? You think I didn't consider that? But my so-called experts told me a blockade might take one or two years to be successful. In the meantime, the Russians could pour down across Manchuria and Korea and invade Japan themselves. No, Major, I know I did the right thing, and I thank you for going on that mission." Truman turned to go back to his desk, then stopped. "Anything I can do for you, son?"

"Yes, sir. I'd like to get back to my unit in the Pacific as soon as possible."

Harry Truman waved one of his military aides to his side. "Colonel Arnold, get this young man squared away, will you?" Shaking Macneil's hand, Truman returned to his duties.

CHAPTER 33

Nagasaki, Japan
Tokyo, Japan
August 9-16, 1945

A B-29 named *Bock's Car* dropped a bomb called the 'Fat Man' on Nagasaki on August 9. It exploded at 11:01 A.M. A member of the bomber's crew—a man of obvious literary bent—was quoted later as saying he "saw a great ball of fire rising as from the bowels of the earth, belching forth enormous white smoke rings."

With only slight exaggeration, the copilot remarked to the bombardier, "That's a hundred thousand Japs you just killed."

The Soviet entry into the Pacific War was remarkable for its exquisite timing. Even as *Bock's Car* was flying toward Nagasaki, the Russians declared war on Japan and invaded Manchuria.

One minute before the 'Fat Man' devastated Nagasaki, where Mrs. Umeko Miyoshi Macneil was living, the six military and civilian rulers of Japan, with the notable exception of the emperor, gathered in an emergency meeting in Tokyo. Prime Minister

Kantaro Suzuki, an admiral bent with age and hard of hearing, began by saying, "Under the present circumstances, I have concluded that our only alternative is to accept the Potsdam Declaration and terminate the war." Others at the meeting, however, wished to continue the fight to the death, so a consensus, always so essential in Japan, was not reached.

Late that same night, the six men met with the emperor in the imperial *o-bunko*. Arguments were presented both pro and con for continuing the war. When it seemed unlikely agreement would be reached, the emperor came to his feet and began speaking in his squeaky voice.

The shocking third sentence from his mouth was, "Ending the war is the only way to restore world peace and to relieve the nation from its terrible distress."

By then, those in attendance realized what was portended. Tears ran down the cheeks of all. Some sobbed convulsively. Even the emperor had to pause and wipe his glasses with the fingers of his white-gloved hand.

"The time has come when we must bear the unbearable," he continued uttering the words that would become the keynote of Japan under Allied Occupation. "I swallow my own tears and give my sanction to the proposal to accept the Allied proclamation. . . . "

Five days later the emperor took to the air to broadcast to the nation Japan's theretofore unthinkable surrender. He used archaic words and the reception was poor, but because they had never heard the Voice of the Crane, the people knew something catastrophic—could it be the nation's surrender to the American and British fiends?—had taken place.

Tears washed over the land of Yamato like a tsunami. In the

subsequent words of one observer, there was probably no other moment in world history when so many people had all cried at the same time.

In a high, uncertain voice, the Imperial Presence made the following announcement to his people:

"After analyzing the present situation
in Japan and in the world, I am forced to
accept the Allied terms of surrender in order
to save my nation from further destruction.
Despite the efforts of the army and navy and
my work over the past four years, fortune was
against us and we are forced to concede victory
to the enemy. The atomic bomb has demolished
our cities and slaughtered our people. I cannot
permit further destruction. . . . I deeply sympathize
with the nations friendly to Japan and with the
bereaved families who lost husbands and sons
and with those who died at their posts in the
homeland.

I advise the people to cultivate the ways
of rectitude, foster nobility of spirit, and work
with resolution to enhance the innate glory of
the Imperial State. . . ."

Among the listeners to this broadcast was the emperor him-self, as he sat in his *o-bunko* in front of a prewar American-made radio. His announcement had been recorded the previous day, the recording hidden to keep die-hard officers from finding and destroying it.

Dr. Chinda Nishikawa listened to the Voice of the Crane in his Tokyo apartment; his home having been destroyed, his wife and children killed. He did not cry, although the concubine at his side shed enough tears for both of them. Turning off the radio, he told her, "Pack your things and go home. Take with you whatever money you can find in the apartment. And take anything else you want. I have no more use—for anything."

There was no fuel for his car, and in any case, his driver had left for a safer climate. It being beneath his dignity at this late date to ride public transportation, he telephoned his office in the Rikken Laboratory. Almost miraculously his call went through.

One of his assistants was on duty.

"You heard the broadcast?" Nishikawa asked. "Good. I think you know what to do. Take the bombs and dump them in the sea. Get word to Konan to destroy everything connected with the project."

"How about the five cyclotrons?"

"Leave them be. They will be useful in peacetime."

"When will we see you, *sensei?*"

Nishikawa cut the connection without answering.

After warming a *tokkuri* of sake, Nishikawa sat on the *tatami* in front of his *tokonoma* and sipped wine reflectively. He was not a man of samurai predisposition. Indeed, with his gnome-like stature and crippled left arm, he might have appeared ludicrous in the samurai image. Nonetheless, his soul contained martial stirrings.

The two principal passions of his life—aside from debauchery—were nuclear physics and oil painting. Nor were his artistic tastes completely incongruous, for there was a traditional samurai fondness for the delicate beside the brutal.

He made his simple preparations: Bring the *tanto,* or short sword, from his sleeping room. Find a piece of white rice paper with which to grip the razor-sharp blade. (The true practitioner never gripped the hilt.) Clear a space where he could kneel facing the Imperial Palace. One final check. It was done.

Chinda Nishikawa gritted his teeth and squeezed shut his eyes. He grunted as the blade entered the left side of his abdomen to a depth of two and a half inches. I have failed in my duty, he thought, and this pain is the punishment I deserve.

Now came the hard part. With a mighty effort, he pulled the blade to the right as far as he could. When it reached a point one inch below his navel, the pain became too intense for him to slice further. He fell forward, knocking aside the easel with its untouched canvas.

At that point, a *kaishaku,* or assistant at *seppuku,* would have severed the head from Nishikawa's body with a long sword, but there was no one to enlist in that role. Consequently, he survived in full consciousness and great pain for three hours and ten minutes.

An hour before the end, Nishikawa spread out the unbloodied part of the white paper with which he had gripped the *tanto.* He crawled three feet and found a brush and a small tube of paint that had fallen from the easel. With blood-glazed eyes, he raised himself on an elbow and wrote, "If only we had been granted a little more time . . ."

CHAPTER 34

Shanghai, China
August 16-17, 1945

Japanese military forces in the Shanghai area laid down their arms on August 16.

In her apartment, Sarah Macneil—aka Lin Hsiao-mai—was joyful. She had heard the news on the radio. She was waiting for Mrs. Chang, but when the amah-san did not appear, Sarah put on a light green summer frock and went downstairs. No one had seen Mrs. Chang since the evening before.

Neither did Colonel Kazuo Ishihara make an appearance at his office. When Sarah arrived, the staff members were milling about, worried and uncertain as to what they should do.

Leaving the office, Sarah rode her bicycle to Pootung. She grimaced in distaste at how much she was perspiring.

No guards were at the gates. Within the center, everything was quiet, although by now it was mid-morning. Surely, they knew what has happened, Sarah thought. Maybe it takes a while for good news to sink in.

She went through three buildings, telling everyone she could find that the Japanese had surrendered and laid down their weapons. Generally, her words were met with disbelief and doubt.

Their indifferent reception dampened her own pleasure at the turn of events.

In late afternoon she mounted her bicycle and started pedaling back to her apartment. She would have a bath and a cold drink. If Mrs. Chang was there, they could talk about what to have for dinner. Who knows, she thought, Kazuo might come by. They could celebrate their survival. He had survived. She had survived, and the Pootung Jews had survived. That was enough to be thankful for.

In her apartment, she removed her damp clothes to prepare for a bath. There was a knock at the door. It might be the colonel, she thought, although he had a key. She donned a *yukata* and opened the door. Two Chinese with grim faces stood before her. One was an officer, the other, an enlisted man. Both were armed.

"Are you Lin Hsiao-mai?" asked the officer, a captain. "We are from General Tai Li's office. You must come with us. Bring your documents."

A chill ran through Sarah Macneil. Tai Li was Chiang Kai-shek's spymaster. How had he got into Shanghai so quickly? It would be a day or two—maybe longer—before Allied forces began to enter the city. Leaflets saying as much had already been dropped on Shanghai. She nodded at the two Chinese. "Let me change," she said.

Tai Li had rooms in the Excelsior Hotel two blocks from Sarah's apartment. Bewildered unarmed Japanese stood about, being watched by Chinese soldiers. Sarah Macneil was shoved rudely into the general's room where he sat smoking on a sofa. Three subordinates stood behind him.

She tried not to look flustered or afraid, though she was. Very.

Tai Li had a thin face and a moustache and cropped hair. He was in uniform with an open tunic. His eyes were bright and black, his lips thin. He spoke slowly and in a low voice.

"What is your name?" He spoke in the Fukien dialect.

"Sarah Macneil."

"Is that one of your several false identities?"

"It is my true identity," she answered in Mandarin.

"Do you have any supporting documents?"

"My American passport is in Tokyo."

"What is that in your hand?"

Sarah wished she had burned her certificate of Chinese nationality. "Oh, this is something a friend of my grandfather's— he was ambassador to China, you know—gave me when I was born. In Peking. Sort of an—honorary citizenship."

"Really? I don't see the word 'honorary' anywhere on this document."

"You could check, you know."

"We have already made inquiries about you."

"Ask Colonel Kazuo Ishihara. He is the—"

"I know who Colonel Ishihara is. We already have him in custody."

"He will tell you. I'm really an American. My name is Sarah Macneil. My father is an American merchant—" She was speaking faster now, and a note of desperation was creeping into her voice. "My mother is Japanese. Her name before marriage was Umeko Miyoshi. I have a brother who is a major in the United States Army."

"We have already talked to Colonel Ishihara about you."

"Well, then. You know, don't you? That I'm an American citizen, I mean." She began to have hope.

"The colonel told us you are Chinese. Your father was Chinese and your mother was a White Russian. Since before the war, you have been working for Colonel Ishihara. Back when he was head of the Japanese secret police in Manchuria."

This can't be happening to me, Sarah thought frantically. "I don't know why he should say such a thing. He knows I'm an American. I swear it's true. Just give me a little time. I'll find a way to prove it. At least until the Americans get here. They'll come in a day or two."

"You have no time. You are a collaborator and a traitor. You will be executed tomorrow morning."

Sarah's mind went blank with shock.

"Oh, by the way, Colonel Ishihara will be executed, too—but not at the same time." Tai Li jerked his head at one of his henchmen. "Take her away."

She was confined to Room 308 of the same hotel. Japanese military people were also being kept, at least temporarily, on the same floor along with hard-to-identify Chinese. Several of the doors along the hallway were open. Six armed guards were on duty. Sarah asked for, and was given, materials with which to write.

Too nervous to lie down, she sat on the edge of the bed. A hundred thoughts thronged in her mind. Escape? Appeals? Seduction? Pleas? Confession? (But confess to what? My God, she thought, what have I done?)

She tried to think rationally. If Tai Li believed she was a Chinese national and had willingly become the concubine of a colonel in the hated Japanese officer corps, she could understand his dislike and contempt. But put her to death? For that? Thousands, even tens of thousands, of Chinese women must have slept with Japanese during the years of the Japanese occupation, so why single her out for this extreme punishment?

In any case, she was not Chinese. If only she had not held on to that damned certificate of honorary citizenship. She had pretended to be Chinese to obtain the position with Colonel Ishihara to begin with, but she told him her true identity later. He, of course, knew the truth, so why did he lie to Tai Li—assuming he did lie? What would it profit him? His punishment was the same whether she were Chinese or Japanese or White Russian or whatever. She had thought he was truly fond of her, had even loved her. Did Kazuo believe her guilt would be less if Tai Li had taken her for a Chinese? — But no; that did not make sense.

Sarah's blood was racing. She could not sit still. Tears brimmed in her eyes. She felt urine overflowing because of her fright. She knew her underclothing was wet. She had nothing to change in to, so she wadded a pillowcase and thrust it between her legs. She had heard fear caused those about to die to lose control of their body functions, and she dreaded the thought of that happening to her. I must have courage, she thought. I am a Macneil. What would Bill say? What would Dad say?

Moving to the small desk by the window, she folded one sheet of paper several times to stiffen it. Then she wrote four words on the strip in large, bold letters.

Setting that aside, she began a letter to her brother, after writing his name, rank, and military unit (ATIS) on an envelope.

Dear Bill,
    The Chinese are going to execute me

JACK SEWARD

tomorrow. They think I am a Chinese national and therefore a traitor. I have racked my brain, but there seems to be nothing I can do.

Therefore, this is to say goodbye and to tell you I love you and all the family.

If you were with me now, I imagine you would ask me something like, "Was it all worthwhile, Chankoro?" (Damn you, I told you not to call me 'Chankoro,' although it does look as if I am going to die a 'Chink,' doesn't it?)

To answer your question, I would have to say Yes. I visited Pootung today and all my Jews were there and alive. That's what I really wanted: to get them through the war safely.

The Japanese have laid down their arms, and the Americans were air-dropping supplies on one of the other detention camps today, although they are not here yet. (Oh, how I pray they will come early tomorrow and rescue me from death. Remember the games we used to play where you rescued me—a damsel in distress—from a "fate worse than death?" Well, let me tell you, brother mine: there *ain't* no fate worse than death.)

I can't say how much good I did for my Jews. I think they might have survived even without me. After all, Colonel Ishihara did much for them, even though now the Chinese say they are going to execute him, too. Even Kenji Doihara was not really anti-Semitic, although, I must admit, he was largely indifferent to their difficulties.

I know I tried to help them in many small ways—ways of which they may not have been aware. I don't expect their gratitude. My reward will come in the next life when I meet Nathan again, and he holds me in his arms and tells me, "You kept your promise, Sarah. You tried to save them. Thank you."

Goodbye, Bill, and love, Sarah.

It was nine-thirty the next morning when the truck in which Sarah and four Japanese officers were riding drove past the Pootung Detention Center. They were headed for the execution grounds beyond the Center.

She could see dozens of the Jewish detainees as they walked among the buildings of the Center. This morning they were more active than yesterday. They were talking to each other with animation. There was vigor in their steps. They seemed like a people in the process of rejuvenation.

For the first time since Tai Li had passed the death sentence on her, Sarah Macneil began to feel a sense of peace. All hope was gone, so she should compose her thoughts. Pootung had faded into the distance, and her Jews were going ahead with their lives. She wished the truck would move more slowly so she could savor these last few minutes. She knew Nathan Blum was watching her and she wanted to make him proud.

With a start, she remembered the small folded piece of white paper on which she had written four words last night. She pinned it to her dress. The other soon-to-die passengers in the back of the truck watched her indifferently. The piece of paper read, "I am Sarah Macneil," and the bold strokes reflected the pride with which they had been written.

There, that will tell them who I am. I hope the bastards suffer some day for killing an American woman who did them no harm.

Later in the day, a Chinese guard in the Excelsior Hotel delivered to General Tai Li the letter Sarah had written to her brother. "The Chinese woman left this in her room," the guard said, after saluting.

"What Chinese woman?"

"Lin Hsiao-mai, sir."

"Who?"

"The woman you sentenced to death."

Tai Li dismissed the guard and opened the letter. His English was not good, and he could not make much of it.

With a growl of disdain, he threw the letter in a wastebasket.

CHAPTER 35

Manila, The Philippines
Atsugi, Japan
Numazu, Japan
August 19-28, 1945

Bill Macneil had no idea what had befallen his sister, Sarah. Had he had even an inkling, he would have done his best to fly directly to Shanghai.

But not knowing, he pocketed his orders and made his way across the United States and then the Pacific to Manila. Without a top travel priority, he was bumped from the MATS aircraft twice en route and did not reach the capital of the Philippines until August 19. There he reported to ATIS headquarters for a new assignment.

His orders must have been flagged "political influence," for he was taken in to see Col. Sidney Mashbir, the ATIS commander, immediately. Still chewing on a cigar, Mashbir welcomed him.

"How are you, Macneil?"

"I'm all right now, thanks."

"What have you been up to?"

"Just taking it easy, sir." Macneil did not know whether the colonel was aware of his surreptitious visit to Tokyo, so he decided to say nothing.

"Well, things are winding down, so what would you like to do next?"

"To tell you the truth, Colonel, I'd like to get back to Japan just as soon as possible."

"I can arrange that, but the question is, in what capacity?"

"It doesn't matter that much, as long as I get there quickly. There's someone in Japan I would—"

"I think I understand, Bill, but I still have to put a tag on you."

"Well, if I'm not presuming too much, maybe I could go with General MacArthur as his interpreter."

Mashbir shook his head. "Sorry, Major Faubion Bowers is already ticketed in that slot." He thought a minute. "You know, we really should have a backup for Bowers. Just in case he comes down with something. How would that be?"

"When could I go?"

"Not on the same plane, perhaps, but right after."

"Suits me, sir. Anything I can do in the meantime?"

"In fact, there is. We're flying in sixteen Japanese officers and diplomats to negotiate the surrender documents. They're due at Nichols Field today. We'll billet them in the Rosario Apartments tonight and convene the meeting in the City Hall tomorrow. Why don't you be there just to keep an eye on the interpreting?"

It didn't take Macneil long to see that negotiations were on the point of rupture. MacArthur's staff had hastily drawn up a surrender document in English and had given it to a team of ATIS translators to turn into Japanese. So far, so good.

But someone on the ATIS team used the standard word for 'I'—that is, *watakushi*—instead of the exclusively imperial word *chin*. It could hardly have been a mistake. Every ATIS translator Macneil had ever worked with would have known better. It was either an oversight, committed in haste, or a deliberate put-down. "Who the hell is this guy Hirohito to think he alone gets to use a special word for 'me'?" someone may have thought.

Faubion Bowers would have known better, but he was not available. From the periphery, Macneil watched as the Japanese delegation turned pale at the implied insult. The head of the delegation, Lt.-Gen. Torashiro Kawabe, shut his eyes and clamped tight his lips in obvious anger. Macneil sensed they were on the point of stalking out of the conference and flying home, if MacArthur would permit them to.

Then they might do what they had been threatening to do all along: arm "one hundred million" Japanese civilians with sharpened bamboo stakes and prepare to repel the Western "fiends" on the beaches of Kyushu and Chiba.

And, as Harry Truman had said, Japan still had some 2,000 kamikaze planes concealed under trees and other camouflage in Kyushu waiting for the invasion fleet.

To say nothing of the atom bombs built by the Rikken Laboratory. Macneil had no way of knowing what might have happened to them, but it was entirely possible the bombs might already be loaded on bombers and ready for takeoff.

He hurried to find Colonel Mashbir. "They've got a problem out there, Colonel."

Mashbir jumped to his feet. "What's wrong?"

"One of our translators must have used *watakushi* for *chin* in the phrase, 'I, Hirohito, Emperor of Japan . . . .'"

"Jesus H. Christ!" Mashbir exploded. "What the shit are they going to do? Pick up their marbles and go home over a little thing like that?"

"You know how they are about things like that, Colonel. You'd better go out there and tell them we'll change *watakushi* to *chin.*"

"I guess I'll have to," Mashbir grumbled, walking toward the conference room. "I just hope Sutherland and MacArthur don't chew my ass out for pampering these goddamned crybabies."

In fact, both Sutherland, the chief of staff, and MacArthur applauded the change Mashbir made when they were informed later.

At dawn on August 28, a fleet of forty-five C-47s circled the airfield in majestic fashion and landed at Atsugi—not far from Tokyo and Yokohama. The first American to descend from the lead C-47 was Col. Charles Tench of MacArthur's staff. Immediately behind him came Major Faubion Bowers, MacArthur's primary interpreter.

Bill Macneil was in the fifth C-47. Most of the arriving Americans stayed at Atsugi, awaiting arrival of advance elements of the 11th Airborne Division and General Douglas MacArthur, who came two days later in a C-54 called *Bataan.*

MacArthur and the advance party, including Macneil, were loaded into prewar vintage black automobiles that ran on charcoal and were driven at a snail's pace the 15 miles into Yokohama. The procession was led, for some reason, by a red fire engine whose forward progress was jumpy and erratic.

More than 29,000 Japanese soldiers lined the road to

Yokohama, all with their backs toward the American arrivals. A *New York Times* correspondent in the same vehicle with Macneil exclaimed, "Dammit, would you look at that? They're turning their fucking backs on us. First thing you know, they're going to drop their trousers and bend over, the bastards."

"Take it easy," Macneil said. "They're facing outward to better protect us from attack or ambush."

The correspondent paled. "Do you . . . think that could happen, Macneil?"

"I doubt it. The emperor has ordered the armed forces to stop fighting, so that's what most of them will do. But there are still some military men out there who would, I'm sure, much rather die than suffer the humiliation of surrender."

The party was assigned rooms in Yokohama's New Grand Hotel, the finest the war-torn city could offer. Before dinner that evening, the Americans were offered beer and other predinner refreshments. Some of the Americans were worried that their drinks might contain poison, although the principal concern of the Japanese hotel staff was that the beer be at exactly the right temperature for their guests.

Bill Macneil, however, did not stay in the hotel to share the beer and steak dinner. He found a rickshaw outside the hotel and hastened to Yokohama station where he caught the first available train to Numazu.

The last time he made this trip—was it only last month?—he was dressed in a Swiss-made civilian suit and wore several yards of bandage around his head. This time there was no mistaking his identity, and he savored the reactions of his fellow passengers. Some averted their faces, some gazed at him with what he took to be admiration, a few bowed slightly. Could any other country in the world be like Japan?

It was full dark before he reached the home of Helma Graf's parents. He prayed she would be there—unharmed. At least there was a light showing in one of the windows.

When she answered his knock, her face turned radiant in an instant. The lovers clung to each other for a long moment. Helma was crying and Bill's eyes were moist, too. He asked her three times if she was really all right, running his hands over her body to reassure himself.

His arms wrapped around her waist, he stepped into the entranceway of the semi-Japanese style house. "I can't stay long, dearest. I'll have to catch the last train back to Yokohama." He explained to her about their arrival at Atsugi and the motorcade to Yokohama. "Anyway, it's all over, Helma."

"What's over?"

"The war, darling. The *war*! You're safe and I'm all right and Ship is with Dad back in Oregon."

She looked faint. "I can . . . hardly believe . . . it, Bill. It's been like a terrible nightmare. I wonder why we survived . . . when so many did not."

Over tea they talked for an hour—until he had to catch the last train. "If I miss it, I guess I'll be the first American in the Occupation to be absent without leave."

"Can't I go with thee?" she asked, clinging to him desperately.

"Not unless you have a place to stay tonight. But I'll be back. I'm in the New Grand Hotel, but I can come back this weekend. What can I bring you?"

"Anything sweet, dearest. I'm starved for sweets. And some real coffee. And . . . oh, yes, butter. Tons of it. And—"

"I'll see what the mess officer can scrounge up for me. Yeah,

I almost forgot. What about Umeko?"

"She survived the bomb, Bill. Isn't that wonderful? All those hills in Nagasaki must have deflected some of the force of the blast."

That, at least, was one bit of good news, Macneil thought.

"I'm sure MacArthur will move his staff to Tokyo in a week or so, and I'll try to find a room somewhere for you—where we can be together. I'll have to keep a room in an officers' billet, of course, but we'll have lots of time together. I'll see to that."

"I pray we will," she said, still clutching his sleeve.

Bill paused in the vestibule to put on his shoes. "Speaking of prayer, Helma—do you think you'll want to do missionary work in Japan again?"

"Never!" she grated with great emphasis.

"Does that mean you would not even want to live here?"

"Not exactly, but I would not want to try any longer to save their souls."

"There are some good Japanese, Helma. We can't forget that."

"Where do thee wish to live, dearest?"

"When the Occupation is over, I was thinking I should rebuild our family business in Japan—and the Far East. I could let Ship run the San Francisco office—and Sarah the one in Shanghai, maybe."

"I will cleave to thee, dearest."

"And I to thee. I mean, to you."

epilogue

The Macneil family was devastated to learn of the execution in China of Sarah Macneil. Bill Macneil made two trips to Shanghai to find her grave but was unsuccessful. During his second stay in Shanghai, he set out to shoot General Tai Li, Sarah's executioner, and had to be physically restrained by officers of the U.S. Army provost marshal. He was forbidden to return to Shanghai during the rest of his military service. After Macneil's discharge from the army in 1949, he made several business trips throughout the Far East. During one of those stays, in early 1950, Tai Li was kidnapped by persons never identified and handed over to the Chinese Communists, who promptly executed him.

Col. Kazuo Ishihara was killed by a firing squad the same day as Sarah Macneil. He was reportedly buried in an unmarked mass grave.

A survivor of the atom bombing of Nagasaki, Umeko Miyoshi Macneil was in better health at the end of the Pacific War than at its beginning. Her stepson, Bill, arranged for her transportation by military aircraft to San Francisco in November 1945, where she was met by her husband Neil Macneil Jr. and her son, Shipton. They purchased a large home near Telegraph Hill, and Shipton reopened the Macneil Brothers' Trading Company branch there.

Under the direction of a team from the Rikken Laboratory in Tokyo, Japanese workers attempted to destroy everything connected with the atom bomb development project in Konan, Korea. Before they were halfway finished with the task, Russian soldiers stopped them and carried back to Russia both the Rikken team and its equipment. What became of them is not known.

On November 28, 1945, American troops dumped into the sea off the Chiba coast, Japan's five costly cyclotrons.

Thanks to new drugs and methods of treatment, Ellen Wood, Bill Macneil's childhood sweetheart, recovered her memory and was able to coherently relate her experiences during the Rape of Nanking. She testified she was repeatedly raped by a squad of eight soldiers, all Chinese. A girl of fifteen at the time, Ellen was unfamiliar with military insignia, but her imprecise description suggested that her rapists were either Chinese Communists or men serving under a Chinese warlord marauding mostly in Honan Province.

At the time of Japan's formal surrender on September 2, 1945, Baron Nobutaka Matsui was living on his estate near Ashikaga. He renewed his acquaintance with many Americans he had known in the United States before the war and became famous for his uninhibited weekend parties. For several years, he rode his horse, Uranus, almost daily. The horse died in 1952, the baron, not long thereafter.

The woman most closely associated with the appellation

"Tokyo Rose," Iva Toguri D'Aquino, was prosecuted by the United States for collaboration with the enemy and sentenced to prison, later pardoned by President Gerald Ford. During the war, she resisted pressure to renounce her U.S. citizenship and was the most outspokenly pro-American announcer of the entire staff at Radio Tokyo.

No charges were ever brought against British Capt. Horace Milmay. He returned to England—and obscurity—in late 1945.

Lieutenant-General Kenji Doihara was tried for war crimes in Tokyo and sentenced to death. He and six codefendants were hanged in the early morning of December 23, 1948. The bodies of all seven were cremated and their ashes secretly disposed of.

Major—later, Lieutenant Colonel—Bill Macneil remained in the army until fall 1949, when he was separated from the service and became a "commercial entrant." He rebuilt the family mansion in Moto-Azabu in Tokyo and resumed the family business. He obtained exclusive U.S. sales rights to a new line of electronic products that became a dominant force in the market.

Helma Graf was married to William Macneil in December 1945 in a ceremony at the Union Church in Tokyo. The couple was assigned a two-story house in Washington Heights, a military dependent housing area in Tokyo, where they lived until Bill's separation from the service four years later.

Following the admonitions of their emperor, the people of Japan "bore the unbearable" and rebuilt their country.

The Author

For 55 years, Jack Seward has specialized in Japan and its language. He has lived in Japan and taught its culture and language in the United States. He is the author of 44 fiction and nonfiction books about Japan.

In 1986, in recognition of Seward's efforts to deepen understanding and friendship between Japan and America, the Emperor of Japan awarded him the Order of the Sacred Treasure. The author lives in his native Texas with his wife, the former Aiko Morimoto, although he still spends considerable time in Japan. The Sewards have two sons, Bill and John.